RADICAL IMPACT

RADICAL IMPACT:
A MANAGER'S PLAYBOOK
TO ACHIEVE
MEANINGFUL RESULTS

BY
ANDY RAY

This book is available for special discounts for bulk
purchases. For more information contact
www.PKFTexas.com.

Library of Congress Cataloguing-in-Publication Data
Ray, Andy.
Radical Impact: A manager's playbook to achieve
meaningful results / Andy Ray
p. cm.
ISBN 978-0-9861704-0-9
2015902264

Book design by
Holly Moxley of Tracking Wonder Consultancy.

Printed in the United States of America

To Ellen, for all the right reasons

CONTENTS

PART 1:
THE STATUS QUO

PART 3:
THE VITRUVIAN YOU

RADICAL IMPACT

INTRODUCTION

WHO THIS BOOK IS FOR

This book is for middle managers. If you aren't the owner, the CEO, or a member of the board of directors, then you are in the middle of your business, and it is a great position to be in.

Middle managers, you have the innate potential to create radical impact in your businesses right now and change the way you work forever. This book shows you how.

FIRE

We live in an age that has within it the potential elements to create a middle management revolution, a golden age of middle management, driven by middle managers creating radical impact, career achievement, and meaningful work. From the early-twentieth century inventions of connectivity such as the light bulb and the telephone to our current age of hyper-connectivity, we have at our disposal an age predisposed to change, and yet the way we manage our businesses is still largely tied to the early-twentieth century Industrial Age way of thinking.

My job for the last twenty years has been to wake up. It's been to wake up first myself, then my staffs, and now my clients from the trance of status quo middle-management performance and launch into the world of radical impact. I am an iconoclast who tears down ineffective management systems and replaces them with systems that work. These systems unleash your potential to create your own radical impact.

I have spent some 40,000 hours in the field, managing companies, managing staffs, and coaching clients. Believe me when I tell you that when I show up at the gates of your businesses and get a whiff of the sulfuric air, I know that I will find most of you in a deep and delusional business trance. The conspiracy of comfort, the false security of conventional wisdom, the candy-coated outdated thinking that today's business entertainers feed you, and the allure of the unattainable "perfect job" has you drooling out of the side of your mouth, dreaming of your next vacation. The status quo has you. You can smell it.

The status quo tricks you middle managers into sleep-walking through incremental results, meager raises, and the hope that someone notices you when Bob retires so that you can get that promotion and the bigger pillow that goes with it. The status quo feeds you trick methodology and gets you to fortify your current company, department, or career status with mind-numbing bureaucracy, staunch defenses of the way things are, and stealthy erosion of your peers' position through courtier politics. As a result, you think that this is what work is, this is what middle management is. You fortify, stack sticks, and stand guard.

But you are being tricked, and you are better than that.

Some of you have walked up the wooden ramparts of your middle management life and peered beyond the fortress of false limitations. You have heard rumors from passersby that beyond the horizon there is a job that means something more than a good nap and hanging in there. You have heard that there are wild tribes of companies and managers that make seemingly miraculous things happen in the land beyond the gates. These roving business operatives burn down the fortresses of the status quo businesses that clog the country side. They charge up their career paths and speed through promotions with the value of their radical impact. And they light up a life of rich meaning in the venture. They howl through the frontier of work life with a battle cry of,

"IMPACT, ACHIEVEMENT, AND MEANING!"

They are the middle management Order of I AM, and they are as real as the planks you stand on right now. They are radical impact-hunting middle managers, and you should be one of them.

You need two things to start the process:

1. Break the spell of the status quo and wake up to the possibility of a rich life of radical impact, achievement, and meaning.
2. And you need a match. This book is your match.

THE FIGHT FOR YOUR LIFE'S WORK

Impact. Achievement. Meaning.

Isn't that what you signed up for when you became a middle manager?

You felt that significant and sustainable impact was within your grasp for your staff, your department, or your business as a whole. You would make it happen.

Achievement in the form of more frequent raises and promotions seemed within range. Your career progression would start to accelerate. You had paid your dues and were in sight of real rewards.

From your middle management chair you would create a balanced life consistent with your values. Your personal time would give you the energy to pour yourself into your work, and your work time would be aligned with your goals and your life vision.

How long did it take for that initial enthusiasm bubble to be popped by the day-to-day reality of most middle managers' work life? A month? A year?

For many of you, your vision of your life's work full of impact, achievement, and meaning was quickly co-opted into a Sisyphean life of pushing stones up a hill of reactive managerial firefighting, babysitting staff, repeating the same daily deliverables, sitting in traffic, squeezing out some vacation time, and waiting for it all to end in a retirement you may or may not be able to afford because the raises and promotions didn't come as quickly as you thought they would, if they came at all.

Your life's work and its meaning had been deferred to your retirement years. Retirement is the time and place where you had hoped you would get your real life's work done, achieve your goals, and live out your life with greater meaning. But in that arc of life, when everything meaningful is deferred to the end, your thirty-year middle-management career was reduced to a great test of character and endurance.

What happened to "Impact, Achievement, and Meaning"?

I'll tell you what happened. It is the same thing that has happened to countless ambitious middle managers before you. The potential of your life's work has been battered by the day-to-day force of a very real, tangible, and active enemy to all that is great in you and in your business. What is this enemy force that works to constantly thwart middle managers' attempts at impact, achievement, and meaning?

The status quo.

The status quo steals the vision you had of your company's future, your department's future, or your career's path, and forces your vision into the mold of the present conformity. It makes you "go along to get along." It dangles retirement years as the prize. The status quo is not a benign force in the business universe. The status quo is a fire-breathing dragon that guards the space between you and the middle management life of radical impact, achievement, and meaning that you are capable of creating. It actively works to kill off any hope, desire, or effort that you will ever exert to do anything meaningful in your business life. It lords over your daily life and works tirelessly to keep you firmly in its hold.

How did it do this to you?

By stunning you when you first started out. The dragon of the status quo kicked your goal of impact, achievement, and meaning right in the crotch and hissed, "Not so fast, rookie. You don't get past me without a fight."

There is only one way to claim the middle management life you are capable of and deserve. You must fight and kill a status quo dragon. Rooting out and killing the status quo must become the driving mission in your middle management life's work.

The status quo is insipid. It has penetrated the business culture you work in and the very conventional wisdom you lean on to solve problems. It has laid traps for you along the way in the form of distracting beliefs that will throw you off the hunt.

In the first part of this book, I show you all of these tricks of the status quo so you will know them when you see them and deal with them with impunity. In the second part of this book, I will equip you with the tools you need to slay it dead.

Fighting the status quo and killing it is the hardest thing in middle management that you will ever do. You would rather train for a triathlon, start a small second income side business, get more degrees, or climb Mt. Everest than stare the beast in your business down and cut its head off. I don't blame you. All those things are easier.

Is that really the you that you set out to be, though?

Don't you sit in the weekly staff meeting and whisper to yourself, "I could fix that problem"? Don't you drive home at night and grumble, "I could do my boss's job in my sleep"? Don't you tell the consultants, "We could have a great company if we could just get the right people"? Over coffee in the morning don't you dream about a job just beyond your grasp that will really kick your career into high gear?

You can fix the problem, do the boss's job, get the right people, kick your career into high gear, and create energy in your life's work.

Who is the real you?

Impact, Achievement, Meaning–I AM.

There's the middle management fight for your life's work.

Will you fight for it?

RADICAL IMPACT

Radical impact obliterates the status quo. When achieved, radical impact is effective one hundred percent of the time against the status quo. As such, radical impact and the status quo are mortal enemies.

Burn this definition in your consciousness. It is your guiding light in the wilderness. Don't let its simplicity fool you.

RADICAL IMPACT happens when a middle-manager creates a significant and sustainable result that matters in a business.

The good news is that the opportunities for you to create a significant and sustainable result exist in every business at all times, and they are the same opportunities in every business. Whether you are a windmill manufacturer or an e-commerce company, a law firm or an engineering business, the opportunities to create radical impact present themselves across all types of vertical industries and business models, because most of those businesses are infested with status quo dragons and, as a result, are underperforming.

Radical impact is foundational, fundamental, and extremely difficult to achieve. The status quo wants you to stay incremental, wants you to optimize and shoot for perfection. It loves wasting your time on tiny progress.

There are five key areas of radical impact opportunity for middle managers that I will detail in Part II:

GROWING REVENUE

OPTIMIZING PROFITABILITY

CREATING CASH

DIFFERENTIATING CUSTOMER SERVICE

INNOVATING PRODUCT OR SERVICE

Are there other areas where you can create a significant and sustainable result in your business? Yes. Too many in fact. The status quo wants to stall you out in the evaluative stage. It throws lots of choices at you, hoping that you will not exert a sustained focused effort in any single one of them long enough to create a significant result. Each of these five target areas for radical impact could be each, on their own, a career's worth of work. They are also slam dunks for radical impact. Focus here and you will create the significant results that matter to your business.

Before you dismiss these five areas as too basic, too fundamental, too boring, ask yourself this question: Have you created a significant and sustainable result for your business in one of these five impact areas in the last year? If the answer is no, then you have come to the right place. What you need now is a sword.

WHAT IS STRATEGIC EXECUTION?

Radical impact snuffs out the status quo every time the two do battle, but how? What is the weapon that deals this perfect and devastating blow to the dragon? It is the double-edged sword of strategic execution in the hands of a master swordsman–a radical impact hunter. Radical impact relies on two absolutes, this weapon and you. There is no radical impact without you, and there is no radical impact if you do not master the use of this lethal weapon of strategic execution. To master use of this lethal weapon you need two things:

1. Technique instruction on how to use this weapon
2. Lots of practice with that technique and the weapon

Over the next few weeks you will develop proficiency in using the sword of strategic execution, and then you will use it to obliterate status quo dragons in your business by creating radical impact. Remember the mission–to annihilate the status quo, that dragon in your business that stands between you and radical impact. The sword of strategic execution, properly applied, will create radical impact. You were made for this.

At face value, strategic execution seems basic and fundamental like breathing. Yet, it is often used incorrectly or incompletely, which limits its status quo-killing power. Ask a yoga instructor to tell you how many of us breathe incorrectly. Even the basics are hard to master. If you use strategic execution incorrectly, you might even hurt yourself or others. Used correctly and completely, however, strategic execution is lethal.

Strategic execution is nothing more and nothing less than deciding what needs to be done in a business that matters, and then getting those things done in a way that creates a sustainable and meaningful result. Remember, that radical impact happens when a middle manager creates a significant and sustainable result that matters in a business. The significant result that matters is the strategy part of strategic execution, and the creation of sustainable results is the execution part of strategic execution.

The power of the day-to-day status quo causes us to wield our strategic execution sword wildly, overreacting or under-reacting to short-term stimulus and the fires the dragon starts. So we employ strategies that have us and/or our staffs working on the wrong "what." We commit time and energy to the urgent rather than the important, and while we may have survived the day in the fort, we have not advanced the hunt toward radical impact. When Peter Drucker quipped that "there is no point in doing well that which you should not be doing at all, "he was getting to the heart of the wild swings that the untrained make at the "what." Instead, as you learn to deploy more technique around the "what," the drain of the day-to-day and status quo distractions begin to fade into the background. You get "ahead of it."

Execution is "how" significant and sustainable results get done, and execution is rarely mastered. Anyone can blitz a problem and create short-term improvement. Yet you cannot sustain a significant result without mastering the execution side of strategic execution. Especially in a larger organization, with a huge appetite for competent talent, "flash" results can be hyper-recognized to the detriment of both the company and the individual, but that does not make them sustainable. Without sustainability, there is no radical impact.

Here's an example. Mitchell was the sales manager of a local branch of a national company. Through a bit of salesmanship and a great regional economy, his branch grew over a one-year period at twice the rate of all the other branches in the company while also improving its profitability. Mitchell was a rock star at the annual branch manager's meeting and as a savvy company politician. He leveraged his great year into a promotion. But his branch results were not sustainable. They were the result of nothing that happened on purpose. Mitchell had gotten lucky. By jumping on this "flash" result, the company 1) sent the wrong message to other branch managers and 2) promoted Mitchell into a position he was not qualified to hold. Within a year after his promotion, Mitchell was fired. Strategic execution creates radical impact, and radical impact is a sustainable result that matters in a business. Sustainability is a key component of the definition that is ignored at everyone's peril.

STRATEGIC EXECUTION is deciding what needs to be done in a business that matters and then doing things that deliver those results in a sustainable way.

Simple, right? So why doesn't everyone just do that? Well, the alphabet is simple. The English language contains only twenty-six letters. We all probably learned the alphabet in our first twenty-four months on the planet. So why haven't all of us written the great American novel, poems that would move us in our soul, or plays that express the human condition? Similarly, numbers are simple. Every number ever built is built with one of ten numbers, zero though nine. So why haven't we all solved the mysteries of quantum mechanics or the secrets of stock speculation? There are twelve notes in the musical scale. Every song we have every known and every symphony, opera or musical ever composed is derived from those twelve notes. Yet, few of us are concert musicians.

There are only three primary colors—red, yellow, and blue. Every masterpiece ever painted or saved photo on your smart phone came from someone manipulating those three colors. You get the idea.

Radical impact is the masterpiece of middle managers. Every radical impact result ever accomplished in business is derived when middle managers effectively wield the sword of strategic execution by answering two questions: "What?" and "How?" The medium, the description, the components are simple to understand like breathing. Mastering the weapon of strategic execution is what makes you a radical impact-creating middle manager ready to slay the dragon of the status quo lurking in your business.

Don't be lulled into complacency by the simple elegance of the weapon in your hand. Mastering strategic execution will take a commitment like you have never exercised before to develop a capability like you have never had before, and it will take a way of thinking and engaging your total self that you may have not considered before. Let's consider that now.

THE VITRUVIAN PRINCIPLE

Leonardo Da Vinci was a master student of his age with a voracious appetite for knowledge. He had an uncanny ability to express his knowledge in a wide variety of media. In 1490, he drew a human figure with outstretched arms, bounded by a circle and a square, on a piece of paper. This drawing was Da Vinci's expression of understanding from the studies he had done on the first century Roman architect, Vitruvius.

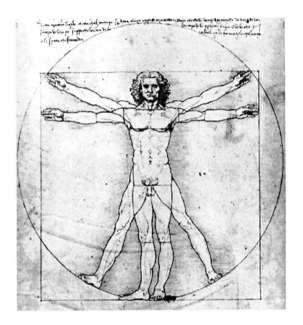

"Vitruvian Man" Leonardo Da Vinci

The drawing Da Vinci produced, "Vitruvian Man," is a masterpiece. It expresses in an elegant and compelling visual blend of two universal human expressions, art and science. Both Vitruvius and Da Vinci were wrestling with and expressing ideas about the natural proportionality that exists in architectural structure (Vitruvius), the human body (Da Vinci) and the universe itself. This proportionality had been explored throughout history by men such as Aristotle and Plato. When this natural proportionality is brought to life through human expression, like Da Vinci's drawing, it creates awe-inspiring truth.

The genius of Da Vinci's "Vitruvian Man" is that the very nature of the drawing itself expresses the truth it is attempting to describe. It is, in its expression, self-evident–a human being is both a work of art and a work of science, perfectly, elegantly, and divinely created. This is the lesson that the universe is constantly trying to send to us through the fortifications of the status quo: There is an elegant, natural proportion, and balance to both the art and science of our humanity. We must use this lesson in our middle management work if we are going to create radical impact.

Why?

RADICAL IMPACT happens when a middle-manager creates a significant and sustainable result that matters in a business.

Radical impact must be created. It is usually not simply a rational extension of some conventional process. Radical impact is not moving the needle from 96.7% to 96.8%. Radical impact is moving the needle for 96.7% to 4,000%. You can't do that without balancing the creative you with the scientific you. You must bring all of you to the radical impact hunt.

Da Vinci's "Vitruvian Man" is the illustration of your human potential expressed through your life's work in middle management–balanced, engineered, and miraculous; logical and wild; curious and true. We can use this simple drawing to inspire a new way of thinking in middle management that obliterates the status quo myth of middle management as compliant rule followers and button pushers. In this one shift in thinking, middle managers can move beyond the limitations of the status quo and tackle radical impact.

Here is the Vitruvian Principle: Middle management is as much an art as it is a science. Therefore, we must employ the entirety of our humanity–both the creative and scientific self–to create radical impact.

The status quo is too strong to fight with half a self. Did your shoulders just drop when you read this last statement? That's the status quo working on you, wanting you to dismiss the idea outright so that you can get back to making nothing important happen. "Creativity?" the dragon whispers. "Flakey, goofy, touchy-feely creativity? Go make a candle; I have a manufacturing plant to run."

I have had many conversations with you on this topic in the field, and they usually start out with you saying something like this: "I am not creative. That's why I got my degree in business." Oh, but you are. Your definition of creativity might just be too narrow. Creativity is not limited to the writer, musician, and painter. Creativity is in the way you raise your children, grow the garden in your back yard, advance the car project in the garage, and manage your career. It's great that you majored in business or even did the work to get an MBA. That experience doesn't exclude you from the creative person you were designed to be. Your business experience focuses your creative potential.

MY STORY

I get your resistance to creativity. I struggled with the same idea. In fact, I spent a decade wrestling with this very notion of creativity and business living in the same body. I intentionally chose not to major in business, though I knew my career would be in business management. I started to pursue a business degree, but I bailed out. I knew I needed a degree to have a shot at anything, so I decided to commit myself to learning to learn. I earned my bachelor's degree in humanities, a degree program that set me on a path to become a business "creative," though at the time I did not know it. At the time, I was a thirty-year-old late-starter, with a wife, two kids, an honorable discharge from the Marine Corps, and a degree in humanities. Some resumé, huh?

My first break came quickly. Early in my career, I spent five years at General Electric where I learned how to manage costs and minimize variation. "Jack Welch's World" was an eye-opener of what could be achieved and what could not be achieved with the conventional wisdom of management's early 20th-century legacy. I moved up quickly, doubling my income, and garnering three promotions in my five-year hitch. But, the tradeoffs for the achievement got out of whack (we moved twice in three years), and I decided to try my hand in the mid-market.

In the mid-market I began experimenting with different management techniques. I focused on developing management teams beyond their occupational duty and into their potential for innovation, creativity, and passion. This experimentation led to different ways to train and structure management teams as a whole, and the results were impressive. I flew through the ranks, achieving C-level status and the rewards that went with it. I was helping the middle managers who worked for me do great work, too. But this was, in reality, only a micro-experiment.

The reality of the majority of middle managers I encountered in companies I worked for and with concerned me. Most middle managers were resigned to the status quo, though they really wanted to do more. Their day-to-day work had been reduced to just a job, a way to keep the lights on. They did their job, not much more. Their life's meaning was away from work, found in family, hobbies, or avocations that had little to do with achievement in the workplace. Their best selves weren't in the office every day. Their job was a drain; their energy came from other places. This is a tragic way to live, pushing the same boulders up the same hills every day, just waiting to get home to the real stuff.

I had spent thousands of hours practicing and succeeding as a radical impact hunter. I had successfully combined performance expertise and creativity into a coaching method that enabled me to coach other people into their own game-changing careers full of impact, achievement, and meaning. How could I translate this work for the millions of business people who wanted more from life?

That guiding question led me to where I am now. I packed a bag and struck out into the world of coaching and consulting.

Now I spend my time coaching you, middle managers. My mission is to empower you to transform your job impact, career trajectory, and life meaning by leveraging the robust combination of business performance expertise and the art of human mastery.

I believe that middle managers are the pivot point of all meaningful business change in the world. And we are in a world desperately needing change. You are the men and women who make everything happen. Mastering strategic execution requires the entire you that you were designed to be–creative and scientific, intuitive and empirical. Radical impact is something you were designed to create. Embrace and develop the Vitruvian You, and you become a radical impact-hunting force to be reckoned with.

How do you start?

Start simple.

THE RADICAL IMPACT CYCLE

The process of mastering strategic execution can be broken down into a six-step cycle that lends itself to a simple pneumonic device. The second part of this book is committed to an in-depth discussion of this cycle. Use it as an instructional guide. There are six steps of the radical IMPACT cycle:

I NQUIRE

M EASURE

P ROTOTYPE

A DJUST

C ODIFY

T RANSITION

The radical IMPACT cycle is comprised of verbs and is always in the present tense. Why? The words are verbs because to transform into a radical impact-creating middle manager you must master each of these six steps in the cycle. You must practice the radical IMPACT cycle like a musician practices scales. You must be able to do them in your sleep. They are present tense verbs because, although you may join the ranks of radical impact hunters and the order of "I AM" when you smoke your first status quo dragon and create radical impact, you are never finished "becoming." Even the most adept of the radical impact hunters continually revisit this progressive radical IMPACT cycle, and you will, too.

How long does it take to complete one journey through the radical IMPACT cycle? It depends on the complexity of the impact you are trying to create. I have seen this cycle completed in one day, and I have seen it completed in six months. The radical IMPACT cycle is a way to sneak attack the status quo; so, the faster you can execute it, the better. More importantly, you must practice and go through the radical IMPACT cycle many times in order to master strategic execution. For your first radical impact hunt, shoot for completing the cycle in eight to twelve weeks. It will feel awkward at first, maybe even uncomfortable, but unlocking the power of this technique cycle and your mastery of it is the key to your ability to create radical impact in any business situation you choose to engage yourself in.

The skills you need to acquire in order to master the radical IMPACT cycle and create radical impact are not the skills most of you have been trained in in your day-to-day business life. You're already a smart, hard-working, play-by-the rules business person. You can't do anything in today's business world without bringing those three attributes to the table. The Vitruvian Principle wakes you up to the fact that in order to create radical impact you must work like both an artist and a scientist. You will use both the tools of Hemingway and the tools of Einstein. You will need this one-two punch.

I can see the sweat forming on your brow. Let me give you two perspectives to help you out. First, creativity is an innate aptitude we are all born with. It is as much a part of your DNA as the ability to see or breathe. This aptitude, when fully expressed as an artist or a business creative, are what make us fully human. This is great news. This aptitude is already within the realm of your human capability. You just have to develop it, and that development happens in the most unglamorous way–through instruction and practice.

Second, while the radical IMPACT cycle is informed by the arts, it is not an art project. It is a way to teach you the business process technique of strategic execution so that you can effectively wield that weapon to create radical impact. Mastery of the radical IMPACT cycle is the secret sauce, informed both by the world of the creative artist and real management sciences.

I will draw examples from the arts, sciences, and the business world to illustrate points throughout the radical IMPACT cycle. I will use these example to help develop the Vitruvian You, but I will always ground the radical IMPACT cycle in its primary mission–to teach you the technique of strategic execution so that you can create sustainable results that matter to your business. Mastering strategic execution is mastering the double-edged sword of art and science in middle management. That is the power of the blade you'll drive through the heart of the dragon.

As you engage the creative and scientific you into the mastery of strategic execution through the radical IMPACT cycle, a Vitruvian You will emerge through the process. It happens through the cycle, not before. The Vitruvian You emerges as a result of your effort, and it is a game-changer for you and your career. You will become a middle manager who is more committed, curious, collaborative, adept at your trade craft, and willing to coach others. In Part III of this book, I describe in depth how to develop five transformational traits. This transformation will change the way you work forever.

SEMPER FI

It is late at night, and eighty men are standing with clean-shaven heads in front of two rows of bunk beds, "racks" in the military nomenclature, waiting to be told to get some sleep. These men are from all different parts of the country, representing several religions and four different races. They have varying levels of intelligence. Some barely finished high school. Others have some college credits. They are large and small, bulky and lean. They did not choose the person they are standing next to. In fact, before this night, they had never met each other. But in that dimly lit barracks, they all shared two things in common: they looked ridiculous, and they wanted to be Marines. I was one of them.

Over the next thirteen weeks these eighty men would endure the crucible know as Marine Corps boot camp. It is a status quo killer of the highest order. I had no business being there, but I absolutely had to be there. I had dropped out of college, had no real job prospects, and no core commitment or capability to do anything substantive about it. I thought that, well, maybe the Marine Corps could help me work that out. I enlisted as flippantly as if I were buying something on sale, "Why not?"

Flash forward thirteen weeks later. I have gained thirty-five pounds and am in phenomenal mental and physical condition. I believe that there is nothing I cannot do with enough commitment and training. I am marching across the parade deck of Marine Corps Recruit Depot San Diego, with thirty five of my brothers in arms, ready to take the beach, the hill, or whatever obstacle stands in the way of our mission. I am a Marine.

Of the eighty men that started boot camp, only thirty five finished together. It is not a typo. I learned later that a fifty-percent drop rate through the boot camp cycle is not uncommon. Why the high attrition?

A few recruits simply could not handle the physical rigor. Their bodies gave out through injury or illness. Of the forty five recruits who did not finish boot camp, only three were lost to injury.

A few recruits self-destructed. The change from civilian to Marine was too dramatic and they climbed the fence or attempted suicide. This group was also small.

What about the other thirty six or so that didn't make it? Were they shot? Did they fall out of a helicopter? Drown practicing a beach landing? Oh, for it to be that heroic. It was none of these. They quit. They refused to do the work that would get them in good enough shape to pass the physical fitness test. They did not engage with the subject matter classes, so they failed their written exams. They sat down, literally sat down, on long runs and had to be picked up and carried into a trailing pick-up truck. In week eleven of boot camp, two weeks before the end, we lost probably twenty recruits.

It was hump week. Week eleven was the week we played war. Deep in the California mountains of Camp Pendleton, we worked on attack drills through the day and force marched through the night. We slept on the ground, when we slept, ate MRE's (the Marine Corps version of fast food), and practiced doing what we were hired to do. The forced marches were brutal, often exceeding eight miles, in the dark, in the steep mountains. This is where we lost the rest of our class. Again, exhausted and beaten, these recruits bailed out by throwing their back packs or rifles down the mountain and sitting down on the side of the road. Many of them, overwhelmed with the gravity of what they had done, wept. They were picked up by the truck, and we never saw them again.

The Marine Corps knows that when a recruit shows up for boot camp he has zero capability. What the Marine Corps relies on is that through their culture, history, and some "gentle" encouragement, the recruit will stay committed to the process long enough for the capability training to kick in. Some do, some don't. As powerful a force as Marine Corps boot camp is, it only wins the battle against the status quo about half the time. It won with me.

Transformation will require both of our efforts. I can teach you the technique of strategic execution in this book, and I can encourage and instruct you in radical impact creation beyond this book. But you must bring a few things to the effort for your transformation to be successful. First, you have to bring enough belief to get you to the next step. Then, you have to stay focused on the process of the radical IMPACT cycle, and, finally, you have to do the work.

FAITH IN THE PROCESS

FOCUS ON THE PROCESS

SUSTAINED EFFORT IN THE PROCESS

Bring these three things to the table, and you will kill your first dragon and become a radical impact hunter, and your fellow hunters and I will gladly welcome you into the Order of I AM. You will be welcomed to a middle management life of impact, achievement, and meaning.

WHAT KIND OF MANAGER ARE YOU?

All change in the world, short of environmental cataclysm, is accomplished through the change created by individuals working alone or in the collective. This truism holds for business as well. Radical impact happens in business when middle managers create it. The initiative is all yours, but you must break from the status quo to exercise it. As you master strategic execution and engage the Vitruvian You in the process, you will transform from the middle manager you are now into a creator of radical impact.

If radical impact happens when middle managers create a significant and sustainable result that matters in a business, then why can't all middle managers do that right now? Because most middle managers have gaps in either their commitment level to the business they work in or they lack the skills needed to wield the sword of strategic execution effectively. Middle managers who create radical impact have high levels of both commitment and skill, and the only way they get that is through practice.

Let's break down what I'm calling you to do with self-assessment. Let me show you four different types of middle managers in the workplace, and you determine where your reference group is. You don't have to share your self-assessment with anyone, but commit to make one break with the status quo right now by being honest with yourself.

LATER DUDE

I was managing a small team of five people, and I had just made my first hire. He was a recent graduate of my alma mater, and I was fired up to mentor this young man into a promising career full of radical impact. On his third day with me, I noticed that he had not returned from lunch. I went to his desk and on his computer monitor was a yellow sticky note with these words: "Later Dude."

I found out through other business contacts that two days into the job he felt that it was a bad fit and he simply couldn't do the work. I don't know what he is doing today.

Just like the Marine recruits whose bodies and minds just won't bend to the rigor of boot camp, some of you are just in the wrong job at the wrong time. There aren't very many of you in this group, but if you are here, you know it in your gut. No one needs to tell you. You have zero commitment to what you are doing or who you are doing it for, and you feel like every day you are wandering around in the dark. Or worse yet, you are self-destructing through some emotional issue or substance abuse problem. If this is you, then please get some help, get stable, and come back to your career when you are well.

You will not move from low commitment and low capability to high commitment and high capability without some serious and dramatic personal changes. When you are low on commitment and low on capability in your work, you are not in a position to make radical impact.

CHICKEN FARMERS

I was coaching a manager in a mid-size company who had concluded that his career had stalled because his president no longer appreciated his effort. Through several discussions and a few onsite observations I had determined that this manager's capability level, at least in his subject matter discipline, was extremely high, but something was missing.

One morning, he was an hour late to our scheduled meeting.

"Sorry," he said, "one of the heaters went out on the barn."

"You have a barn?" I asked.

"I have three."

"Why do you have three?"

"The chickens."

He raised chickens as a side business for one of the big chicken processing companies in the area. The barns are really called "hot houses" in the chicken-raising business, and they must stay warm. I am a city guy. The only thing I know about farming and animals is what I heard from my grandparents or parents: Farm work is really hard work.

"This time of year those birds keep me pretty busy," he said.

"How many chickens do you have?" I asked.

"About sixty thousand."

I discovered his career problem.

I advised him, in no uncertain terms, that if he wanted to get his middle management career back on track he had to commit to it whole-heartedly. It turns out he had missed a lot of work with various poultry problems, and even when he was at work he was either exhausted or too distracted to get much proactive work done. His president wasn't the problem.

How many of you are juggling your life outside of work with your life inside of work? This is the status quo whispering in your ear the distracting belief of an illusory work-life balance. Or how many of you, with all the capability in the world, are mailing it in everyday because in your mind the bargain has gotten out of balance with your boss or the company you work for? This is the status quo working on your ego.

There is a price to be paid to make for the personal transformation you need in order to create radical impact. It does not happen in wishful thinking or sitting on your hands waiting for your business to get things right with you. It happens when you apply commitment and capability with abandon. That means a lot of sustained and focused effort plus a real-time commitment.

If I asked you right now to give ten to twenty hours a week over the next three months to radical impact creation, would you do it? Could you do it?

Between your personal life, your hobbies, your energy level, your work ethic, and your sense of a fair bargain with your business, you have been lulled into believing that hanging in there is adequate. Transforming from the "status quo you" to the "radical impact you" will be one of the toughest transitions you will make in your life. It is far more difficult than Marine Corps boot camp, but it is the critical step you must make to join the order of "I AM" and live a middle management life rich with impact, achievement, and meaning.

The good news is that you can make a decision and shift your level of commitment. It's easier than you think, and it is all on you. Don't wait for the business to get right with you. It never will. With commitment and your existing subject matter expertise, the move to radical impact becomes about practice and instruction in the radical IMPACT cycle and the mastery of strategic execution. If you wait for the business to get it right for you then, well, you are roosting.

"Sell the chickens," I told him. "That's how you will get your career back on track."

"I am not going to do that," he answered. "Those chickens are my future."

He never saw it, that those chickens weren't really chickens. They were status quo dragons, and he had sixty-thousand of them dragging him into barns behind his house.

How many do you have?

FORT BUILDERS

Most of you are fort builders. You have been led by the dragon to focus on defense of the status quo of your company, your department, or yourself. You have built a fortress around it all, what you do, who you are, your role in the big picture. Of course, you have been misled into believing that the path to "Impact, Achievement, and Meaning" is to hold the fort rather than take new ground by killing off the status quo.

Sure, there are pep rallies at the end of the year, everyone gathered around the fire, pumping each other up with next year's goals and objectives. Chest-beating proclamations of how "Next year will be the year we go out there and conquer our market and our competition!" We may even swing the gates of the fort open for a while and let the fresh air of change into our citadel. This is what you do when you ask me or other consultants to come in and stir things up.

But after the enthusiasm of striking out on an adventure wears off and the reality of the cost of such an adventure sets in through risk evaluation, the gates close, the fire is stamped out, and you look at each other and decide that what you are really good at, the prudent thing to do, is to build stronger, higher, and thicker walls. And this is exactly what that beast of the status quo wants you to do. It keeps you away from him.

It is not your fault. It is how you were trained to work. You were told that if you showed up every day, followed the rules, worked hard, and were good at what you did, that good things would follow. You would have a job for life, firmly planted in the middle class and, in the words of John Mellencamp, "vacation down at the Gulf of Mexico." That was the American industrial model of the middle management behavioral code that most of us were catechized into. The fortress started crumbling in the late-twentieth century when the rest of the world showed up and decided that they wanted to be industrial, too, and they would do it cheap, cheap, cheap.

Now, compliance, conscientiousness, and competency get you in the door and not much more. You can't build a company, department, or career on them anymore, unless you just want a fort. Stroll through Europe's countryside or the American West, and observe the number of obsolete or obliterated versions of state-of-the-art forts built from the middle ages through the nineteenth century. They all have one thing in common. They are obsolete. The effort and engineering it took to build them is irrelevant. They simply do not matter anymore. They are relics of a status quo approach. It's time to quit defending turf and strike out to the frontiers of radical impact. Yes, you expose your rear to political moves. Yes, you risk failure of your mission and the ensuing chastisement that comes from fort builders who secretly envy those who travel beyond the gates. Here's the thing. No one ever got anywhere holding ground.

If you can muster enough courage to strike out beyond the gates, then you can develop the capability you need to beat the dragon. But you will never develop the capability if you don't throw yourself out there.

If you have solved showing up, working hard, and developing core competency, then you are miles ahead of the "later dudes" and the "chicken farmers." Radical impact for you is all about improving capability.

Your first step is not even as risky as leaving the fort. Your first step is to mentally change your reference group. Mentally leave your fort-building peers. Get your head up and shift your perspective over the walls of the day and to the horizon of possibility. Go up to the roof if you have to. Your fort-builder peers will be no help to you in this transition. In fact, they will work against you. They will tell you that you are a dreamer, you are arrogant, you are a suck up, a brown-noser, not part of the team. When you hear that, be encouraged.

It's not what you hear that will move you forward. It's what you will see.

RADICAL IMPACT HUNTERS

"Impact, Achievement, Meaning!" This is the battle cry of the Order of I AM and of the elite breed of middle managers, Radical Impact Hunters. These are radical impact-generating business marauders. They roam the horizons of their business seeking out the dragons of the status quo, and they obliterate them. They don't co-opt them, collaborate with them, get "buy in" from them, or win them over. They smoke them, wiping the status quo from the face of the earth forever.

They are the courageous who venture out from the false comfort of the farm and fort because they know that the farm and the fort are one hot breath away from destruction. They are courageous because they know they can fail, but they fight anyway. Setting out to the frontier of business, to hunt down the status quo and kill it, is dangerous. Of course, for most of you, it is not a literal life-and-death situation, but it can be no less unnerving.

When you set out to break from the pack and commit to radical impact hunting, you are exposing yourself to your fear of failure. That takes courage, and the reality is you will fail along the way. You need to fail, in smaller risk battles, so that you can build your impact-hunting chops for the big stuff. This is why you need to engage the fullness of your human potential, the Vitruvian You, the creative and the scientific.

Radical impact hunters know they can't kill a dragon straight up. That would be foolish. They are rooted in the foundational knowledge they need to be adept, but they don't stay there. They know that dragon-killing is not going to be learned on Wiki-anything or found on Google. It is their creative use of their own wits that wins the day. Their creativity would not allow them to live long among the chicken farmers and fort builders.

Radical impact hunters are the committed middle managers who kill dragons or get killed by them. There is no returning back to the farm or the fort from whence they came. For them, it is kill or be killed. Their commitment is nearly religious.

Radical impact is a difficult thing to create. There will be major obstacles, as the status quo tries to torch you at every step. If you are not committed, if you have retreat plans or exit ramps built up in your mind, then you will shrink at the first onslaught of heat. It takes enormous commitment to develop yourself into a radical impact hunter.

Here's the good news: Every radical impact-hunting middle manager was once a chicken farmer or fort-building middle manager. None of them, not one, were born radical impact hunters. They were compliant, conscientious, and competent. The only difference between them and the chicken farmers and fort builders is that they stood up one day and heard or saw or felt the call of "impact, achievement, and meaning," and they stepped beyond the gates, burned their farms and forts down, and set out to the horizon. They did the work and honed their strategic execution skills, and they became lethal.

What's the payoff for this life choice? Radical impact-hunting middle managers know that as they develop expertise in status quo dragon-killing they become an invaluable member of the business world. This skill brings with it dramatic achievement opportunities both in compensation and rapid career progression. When you are a radical impact hunter with "skins on the wall," you are always in demand and you will always draw a compensation premium over your chicken-farming and fort-building peers. This impact and achievement feeds their sense of meaning because they are doing both work that matters and reaping the rewards for the effort. Radical impact-hunting middle managers have unlocked the secret of work life, that achievement and meaning always follow impact.

What is it that separates these dragon-killing radical impact generators from the pack?

They have extended themselves beyond compliance and into the courageous. They have embraced the Vitruvian Principle and have become balanced business creatives and scientists. And they have reached beyond conscientious duty-bound work and have achieved total commitment.

How did they do it?

Through mastery of strategic execution that is practiced through the radical IMPACT cycle.

This is great news because this victory is within your reach. You can learn how to create a significant and sustainable result that matters to your business. You can become a radical impact hunter through nothing fancier than learning good technique and practicing it.

At the beginning of the book I told you that you needed two things to begin the process of joining the Order of I AM. You needed to wake up to the possibility of life beyond the fort, and you needed a match. That starts the process. When you take those two steps, you have enlisted. Now we shave your head and start the hard part, battle training.

To join the Order of I AM, to be a card-carrying member and learn the secret handshake, you have to accomplish one thing. Kill a dragon.

This is no small feat. It took Hercules to kill the Hydra in Greek mythology and Hercules was the son of Zeus, the highest god in the Greek order of things. It will take no less of a Herculean effort for you to kill your first dragon. The status quo is that powerful.

It's time you got to know your enemy.

RADICAL IMPACT

PART 1:
THE STATUS QUO

The enemy of radical impact is the status quo. The status quo is a fire-breathing dragon that hides in every break room, cubicle, manufacturing facility, distribution center, company car, and boardroom. Its mission in life is to keep everything the same, and it is ruining your career, your company, and your life.

The status quo has spent a century stripping business culture from its human potential and devolving it into the anemic relationship that now exists between most businesses and their middle managers. As if that weren't enough, between where you are now and the radical impact you will create, the status quo has erected a labyrinth of myths and self-limiting beliefs to thwart every step you make toward radical impact. There are hundreds of these myths and beliefs, and they evolve with enormous speed into the vocabulary and context of every business trend and fad as soon as the status quo can whip them up. I will cover the biggies here.

You will, of course, defeat all of these myths when you master strategic execution. I place this enemy intelligence briefing first, before the radical IMPACT cycle, so that you know what you are dealing with. You must recognize the status quo, the enemy, at every step. By gaining enemy intelligence, you can achieve an early advantage, and you will need every advantage you can get.

ONE:
THE LAY OF THE LAND

We have come a long way since the early days of the Industrial Revolution. In the beginning of the Industrial Revolution, children were considered a viable labor source, pay was highly discriminatory, and work place safety was never a consideration. In the early days of the industrial revolution, near the end of the 19th century, people died at work. At least, in the Western world, those days of all-out human exploitation are fading into the distant past. However, it is important to note that all those changes that removed children from the factory floor created a fair day's pay for a fair day's work, kept the facility from burning down around you while you worked, and were hard-fought victories from the reformers of the day.

The lesson for us in the modern world of middle management is that big business, as a dispassionate entity, does not morally exist to do the right thing. It exists to make money for its ownership. As such, a large business or corporation generally has no intrinsic motivation or genetic structure to provide middle managers with a fulfilling life of impact, achievement, and meaning. That life must be attained the same way every individual benefit from the industrial world has ever been attained–through a hard fight with the status quo.

I deliver this tough news because since the mid-1970's there has been a perceptual shift in Western business to create a weak illusion that business, as a dispassionate entity, is much more attuned to your needs and that, if you will just fall in line, the company will see to it that your contentment is paid for. This message is an anesthesia, and you know in your gut that it is false. Yes, some modern businesses do amazingly good work in the world. They produce goods and services of real value to society. And, yes, some companies work to empower their middle managers and employees. But those examples remain the exceptions.

This tough news and view is not meant to be cynical. It is aimed to reorient you.

Your fighting chance for a life of achievement, impact, and meaning happens when you make it happen. Your business will not make it happen for you. This tough news is good news because it puts you in control of what happens next.

IS YOUR BUSINESS PULLING FOR YOU?

Big businesses need you to think that you are a critical part of the equation, that your health and happiness is as important to the company as the bottom line. But it is not. I have been in too many closed-door executive team meetings for me to believe that your business considers your best interest very much at all. Your business is not pulling for you. Nobody is pulling for you unless you are a radical impact creator. Then, your business will move heaven and earth to keep you "happy."

Think about the innocuous term "human resources." HR is where we go if we have a pay or benefits issue, or if we want to complain about the boss. But by its very title, "human resources," it puts you in your place. You are a resource, like raw materials, office supplies, or energy. You are a resource to be used until your yield declines beyond usefulness. You are, therefore, a cost to be contained and leveraged.

Your business does not want to give you a raise, promote you, or have you stand out in anyway. That would cost more. It will tell you it wants you to stand out. At the Christmas lunch it will throw around some bonuses and coffee shop gift cards to recognize people in order to advance the perception that it is pulling for you. But it is perception management.

The CEO does not stroll through the halls looking for his next protégé to pluck out from the cubicle farm and develop. Your boss doesn't do it either. And if you are the typical boss, you are probably not pulling for anyone yourself either.

I have seen too many years wasted deep in the organization chart by smart, good-hearted middle managers who remain in dead-end jobs out of loyalty to a company, an owner, a CEO, or a boss because they believe that someone in the company is pulling for them and has their best interests at heart. The reality is that business loyalty is a day-to-day proposition. Very few employment contracts exist in the rank-and-file staff.

In your business, you are the only one pulling for you. You own your career and its advancement. You own your raises, your bonuses, and your lifelong income. You determine it, choose it, and create it. Since your business is not really pulling for it, you do not owe it loyalty to longevity but to performance only.

If the equation of career reward to loyalty gets out of balance, you are free to pursue radical impact elsewhere. You own it. You are it. You decide where to hunt.

DOES YOUR BUSINESS VALUE YOU?

As a director in General Electric, I personally laid off a dozen people in a week. Why? To get cost in line and make the bottom-line target our division had been challenged with making. We were not losing money. We just weren't hitting the target. In GE, managers got replaced for not hitting targets. In this kill-or-be-killed world, the layoff was a quick way to hit a bottom-line target. It was so ingrained in GE managerial methodology that there was a saying that made its way through the middle management culture: "There is no bad time for a layoff." You are a cost to the business you draw compensation from.

In many businesses, "people" cost is one of the highest if not the highest cost line on the income statement. The bigger and more public the company is the more this "people" cost is scrutinized. When a business's profitability struggles, cost comes out first, and often, this means you. Rather than re-tasking, re-focusing, re-prioritizing or re-visioning a staff toward radical impact, many businesses make their income statements whole by subtraction, cost subtraction, people subtraction.

In twenty years of managing, consulting, and coaching businesses, I have never seen a non-bankrupt business lay off a radical impact-creating middle manager. If you are creating sustainable results that matter to your business, you are a prize member of that business team. Yes, you are still a cost, but you have a clear, definable return on that cost that blows the math in your favor. You create the value that a business pays for. Businesses will always pay for value. In a turbulent economy, the number one thing you can do to create long-term employment and personal economic success is to make the value equation crazy for the business you get paid from. Big businesses value your results. Create radical impact, and the equation will always be in your favor.

DO YOU HAVE TIME TO GET BETTER?

You don't. Let me get that out on the table right now. Most of the middle management "slack" that would allow middle managers time to work "on" their businesses and not just "in" their businesses was stripped out during the recession of 2008. You barely have enough time in your day just to get the work done you have to keep your team moving to the next day. I sit with middle managers and management teams and help them chart a radical impact path for their businesses, divisions, or departments. Repeatedly, their initial assumptions are that their staffs have plenty of time to work on radical impact creation. Then I go down stairs to meet with staffs, and collectively they tell me that the managers are nuts.

Read any book on improving anything in your business, and many of them make the same assumption–that you have time to do any of it. I have been with you while you eat at your desks and put in ten-hour days (or more). I have taken your calls and emails while you work on Saturdays and at home after the kids are asleep, and I can see that you are treading water, barely, trying to fight off the wave of the day-to-day. You don't have time to work on creating radical impact. No matter what the bosses think, you just don't. The frustrating part is that you know as a middle manager that this project you have been assigned will not have that much impact, if it is even accomplished at all. For you, it's all a big waste of time you don't have.

Here is where you need to shift your thinking. You don't have time if it is someone else's impact project coming at you. Your time is best spent when you proactively identify, work, and deliver your own radical impact work. That is the key. That is where you will find fifteen minutes here and there. That is when you will delegate or cajole peers into helping more effectively.

Every artist and business creative struggles to find time to create something radical. Get stingy with your time. Say "no" or "later" to other projects or initiatives as often as you can for a while so that you have time to work on the radical impact you identify and decide to tackle. When you own the thought process and dispel the status quo's view of the lay of the land, you become empowered.

YOU ARE THE ONLY ONE PULLING FOR YOU

YOU CREATE VALUE THAT A BUSINESS PAYS FOR

YOU MUST USE WHAT TIME YOU CAN ON YOUR OWN RADICAL IMPACT CREATION

Now you are working in reality, the veil of dragon smoke lifted, and you are ready to set out on the hunt. Let's make sure you have the right maps in your back pack.

TWO:
THE FOUR MYTHS
OF CONVENTIONAL
WISDOM

The status quo cozies up to conventional wisdom and wraps it up in a warm blanket. It passes this conventional wisdom down from generation to generation so that when you buy into it in your business life it seems as if you have known it forever. The dragon of the status quo concedes that, in its day, conventional wisdom slew some dragons, but that is old news. Conventional wisdom is handed to you masked as a reliable set of navigational maps that can lead you to radical impact, but it won't. What we know as today's business conventional wisdom was largely formed by early twentieth-century industrialists. Most of what we read or listen to now is a rehash of a fifty-year-old theory and knowledge.

To stay true to your journey and arrive at the destination of radical impact, you need revised maps that will help you use the valuable parts of conventional wisdom and discard the rest.

#1: THE MYTH OF BUSINESS EDUCATION

Should you get a bachelor's or master's degree in business?

Like all good business challenges, the answer is a little yes and a little no. No doubt, getting up to speed in the language and concepts of accounting, economics, finance, business law, and statistics is foundational to sound decision-making in a real-world business environment. It is also critical that most of you attain, at least, an undergraduate level of collegiate education so that you will have a shot at jobs that have that requirement in the job description. You will be eliminated at the resume review stage of every job that requires a college degree if you do not have this box checked in the initial application. Is this fair? No.

I have personally worked with some brilliant business leaders with little or no college-level education. I have also worked with some folks with master's degrees from prestigious universities that couldn't manage a business out of a paper bag.

Middle managers work for the folks that are starting and running companies. In those companies a human resources professional scans, or has software scan, hundreds of applications and resumés for every job opening. In order to fill the job, they must first eliminate applicants. They are not searching for the best applicant in the initial review. They are searching for those that don't meet the basic requirements. The status quo has these HR folks by the ear.

"Just get through the work." The status quo whispers.

And so the folks without the degrees get tossed.

Fair or not, you won't get the look without a degree. But should it be a business degree?

In 1911, Fredrick Taylor published *The Principles of Scientific Management.* Business leaders and academia flocked to this book and to Taylor's work as a way to elevate the practice of running businesses to a science, a real science. Business schools were created to teach this new science. These were top-notch schools like Harvard, The University of Pennsylvania, and Dartmouth.

Scientific management became the dominant conventional wisdom of the age, and for a time it had real and significant impact. Then came the dragon, and in the shadows of the good part of scientific management he created a myth. "Science can solve all of your management challenges," it whispered. This myth cozied up alongside conventional wisdom and fostered a closed loop system of schools, degrees, consultants, alumni, and followers committed to scientific management that was designed not to create radical impact, or help you, but to defend this new status quo to the teeth. The people in this closed-loop system were good people trying to do good work, but they had been sucked into the myth that science could solve all business management challenges. Once they bought in, they were zealots.

Taylor's work was followed by Elton Mayo's work. *In 1933, The Human Problems of Industrialized Civilization* argued that managing the people side of the business equation was as important as managing Taylor's "one right way" or scientific process approach to business management. Mayo conducted the famous "Hawthorne" studies to get in line with the scientific approach to management, and Mayo's school of "human relations" were co-opted by the status quo as the way forward in management. Taylor's process approach combined with Mayo's human relations approach remained the center of the management science universe through the first half of the twentieth century.

Then in 1964 Peter Drucker published *Managing for Results*. Drucker's work focused on the importance of strategy and organizational design. The hierarchical organization chart that most businesses still rely on today was formalized by Drucker in an age when phones were plugged into the wall, computers were the size of your garage, and many women were still discouraged from working outside the home or schoolroom. Your strategy sessions and perennial obsession with planning was Drucker-influenced.

All of this management knowledge, resting on the work of Taylor, Mayo, Drucker, has become the foundation for almost all formal undergraduate and graduate business education. Three schools of thought cobbled together as an accepted unified theory of business management. Look at any business curriculum in any university and you will see these three men's influence firmly entrenched.

When you see any college course on logistics, operations management, supply chain management, inventory management, Lean, Six Sigma, or total quality management, you are in the world of the "perfect process" created by Taylor.

When you see a course dealing with organizational behavior or human resources issues, you are in the world of "human relations" created by Elton Mayo.

When you see a course on organization design, structure or strategy, you are in the world created by Peter Drucker.

Those of you who have logged anytime in real world business management know that there is no such thing as a general theory of scientific management that is universally applicable, testable, and repeatable. That map of conventional wisdom has been dulled by an increasingly volatile world full of uncertainty, complexity, and ambiguity. Your business management challenges are too specific, and your impact solutions are nearly always custom jobs. Conventional wisdom does not a reliable map make because it leaves out the most powerful force for radical impact in today's business world. You. Do you need to knowledge of the rubric of conventional wisdom? Yes. You need to know the old map to read the new map. The knowledge in conventional wisdom is useful. Do you need to acquire this knowledge through formal business education? No. You can self-teach all of what conventional business wisdom has to offer. And your expertise as a radical impact hunter will be far more efficiently attained through real-world practice, rather than sitting in a classroom.

#2: THE GURU MYTH

The dragon knows that a few of you will summon up the courage to venture beyond the farm and the fort. So, it has countered your courage with a group of map makers to waste your time and effort and, ultimately discourage you from the journey toward radical impact.

It is a reflexive response for many of you. I know it has been for me. No matter what the business challenge, the knee-jerk reaction is to hop online and see if there is a book on the subject. It is probably where you found this book.

This is the great age of access, and as an autodidact I can tell you that this has been a lifesaver for me in many a pinch.

But the dragon in the shadows uses this quest we have for unknown knowledge and creates an industry designed to keep us stuck in our pages, seminars, and facilitated meetings, and out of the real work of radical impact creation. This is the industry of the business guru and the myth comes to you in a smoky whisper from the dragon as you comb through the pages of the latest book in your search for a path from good to wherever.

"You have no idea what you are doing," the dragon whispers. "But these gurus do. They know all, see all, and are devastatingly entertaining aren't they? Why don't you shut down for the day, the weekend, the week, the month, the quarter and see what these people have to offer? Then, when you know how to emulate them step-by-step, then, it will be time for you to get to work on your 'problem.' Unless, of course, there is another guru with an even more dazzling array of buzzwords and mnemonic devices, then check them out too, before you get too far down the road of not knowing what you are doing."

Every one of the countless speeches and "pump-me-up" seminars I have sat through gave me a sugar buzz, inspired me, and made me feel like I could conquer the world, until I got back to the real one. In the heat of the dragon's breath, it is your capability and commitment that wins the day. That capability and commitment has very little to do with how fired up you are in the short term.

Business gurus come in three flavors. There is the guru's guru, who writes some wildly popular book that sets up a branding blitz that can last for years. Then there is the celebrity executive that also leads with a book about how if you would just do things the way they did to turn company "X" from a frog to a prince, then you could turn your company from a frog to a prince, too. Finally, there is the celebrity in one field that cross-pollinates their domain expertise from his field into business. This is the famous basketball coach who can teach you how to lead a business by mastering the team in "motion," or the astronaut who wants to teach you how to see the big picture of your business in "orbit." Business gurus can be both helpful and instructive. The problem comes in when we become hooked to the sugar buzz, and we abandon our own instincts, or, worse, our own real effort.

I am here to give you a pass on expert knowledge. You don't need to have any idea of what you are doing to begin the journey toward radical impact. Radical impact is achieved through sustained and focused effort, not sustained observation. You have no idea what you are doing and you won't until you do it.

Read one book on your specific challenge, then get to work.

#3: THE MYTH OF THE NEW

Every step you take to get "you" back into the equation of business radical impact will be met with a disproportionate amount of status quo force against you. That force is designed to make you stop. Even after you have broken free of the guru cycle, read your one book on the subject matter of your business challenge and are ready get hands on and heads up, the status quo makes its move.

Not yet," the dragon says, "I'll concede that you have something going here. But, before you dive head in to this 'effort,' why don't we make sure you are not going to waste a lot of time covering ground other people have recently covered. Why reinvent the wheel? Surely, someone has just solved this problem before. You live in an age of hyper-connectivity. The human brain has extended itself into an endless range of search algorithms and digital solutions. There must be an answer there, in the new."

Knowing that you are, by now, becoming suspicious of the status quo's influence, it hits you in the gut. There must be a best practice, someone has just come up with, that you can emulate. Why don't you call in a consultant and see what they have to say? After all, you don't want to look silly.

The myth of the new says, "Everything changes so fast, and human accomplishment is accelerating, so find the newest path. It will get you to your destination." So if you will search or socially network or find the newest best practice or the latest app, you will find the solution. This is a powerful myth. Even though all radical impact solutions are custom jobs, we are continually lulled into the trap of our age–connect and search for the new. The resources available for radical impact hunters in this age of connectivity are impressive. We have at our disposals more information and more people to help us than in all of human history. The status quo wants you to use these resources to be enamored with connecting to the new. In that way, you will be on a continuous search for the path and will avoid the real work of creating radical impact.

Radical impact hunters must travel beyond the land of apps, Google searches, best practices, and of "liking" new social networks, because, quite frankly, they don't believe best practices are best anything and they know that radical impact is not tweeted. Radical impact is created when the dragon of the status quo in a business is obliterated, and not until then. The map you need is not in the new you find online; it is in the new that you create. That is the map forward. Let others find you in their search.

#4: THE LONE WOLF MYTH

Since you are getting dangerous, the status quo hurls the kitchen sink at you. You are getting too close to ignoring its biggest weapon, conventional wisdom. You are getting too smart for your own good and are able to see the dragon in the shadows. "Fine," the dragon huffs. "You want to do this thing? You want to burn down the farm and the fort and become this radical impact hunter–which by the way–goes against everything you have been taught. You want to explore the 'art' of management, and abandon the gurus? You think you can come up with something new, something radical? Fine. But you will have to do it alone."

Especially in the United States, we prize the individual. Our very founding was based on the elevation of individual rights and freedoms. Throughout our existence as a nation and a culture we have exalted those individual "pull up your boot straps," "roll up your sleeves," "burn the midnight oil," individuals, who through hard work and dogged determination break through the crushing weight of the collective and rise to wealth, fame, and prominence. This cultural fetish with individual achievement permeates our American business culture. We love the celebrity executive who did it his way (still rarely "her" way). We comb through the organizational chart to find the top performers. We give plaques to the hardest of the hard workers. I have been in companies in which staffs will not leave the office at the end of the day just so they can create the appearance of hard work and effort.

Here's the thing. For you to be a great radical impact hunter who creates sustainable results that matter, you must be an incredibly strong individual. Moving from chicken farming and fort building to radical impact hunting will transform you as an individual business force, but you cannot create radical impact alone. The lone wolf starves on the path.

To be successful in your journey, you must collaborate on three axes.

Unless you are the CEO or the owner of your company, then the very first axis you must learn to collaborate with in order to create radical impact is the "up" axis. If you are in a small or midsize company, the "up" may be the CEO. If you are in a large company, the "up" will be the manager, director, or executive one level above you on the org chart. At the very minimum, your "up" must buy into your radical impact journey because she will need to allow you time and resources to make the transition. You can't create radical impact in a vacuum. You must create it in your live business. Without "up" support, you don't stand a chance. You may be fortunate enough to have an "up" that is a radical impact hunter in her own right. If so, you have hit a developmental gold mine. Without being a drain on your "up's" time, you can lean on her to coach and mentor you through your radical impact transformation. If your "up" is a true radical impact hunter, then coaching you is in her or his DNA anyway. The trick is that they will always wait for you to engage them.

If you are a supervisor of any number of staff, whether it be three people or three hundred people, you will also have to master collaboration with the "down" axis. This is where your individualism and the myth of the lone wolf will really gnaw at you. You must delegate so you can focus on your best efforts. You will not create radical impact if you do not engage, to its fullest extent possible, the collective effort of your staff. At its lowest level, you must delegate tasks that eat up your time in low-value tactical troubleshooting, fire fights, or whack-a-mole problem-solving. At its highest level, your staff is a force multiplier of radical impact ideas and solutions. Fully engaged by you, you can accomplish incredible things, but you must do the work to pull them into the radical impact transformation.

Finally, most radical impact journeys find their way into cross-functional solutions. A revenue improvement journey might need accounting help. An operations journey might need IT support. By definition, radical impact must be sustainable. For that you are going to need the help of other functions inside your business. To do that, you will have to collaborate horizontally, across your managerial level of the organizational chart. Of the three collaborative axes, horizontal collaboration is the hardest one to pull off. Everyone is busy, and getting the IT guy to pull ad-hoc reporting so that you can move your "little" project forward can make you feel like Oliver Twist asking for another bowl of soup. Collaborating and engaging the turf holders in your business is tricky and best approached with a degree of humble confidence. Yet without those other teams engaged, you won't sustain the impact of many hard-won victories.

The American myth of the lone wolf will not work, and has never really worked, in the world of middle management radical impact. Your new map to radical impact will guide you through villages of would-be collaborators. Take the time to sit around the campfire with them. They are essential to your journey's success.

With these new maps of lifelong learning, moving without knowing, creating the new, and collaboration, you avoid the old worn paths of conventional wisdom that the status quo has given you to keep us from sticking to the journey. Your new maps are powerful tools, and the dragon shudders when even a single individual pulls this new guidance from his back pack. Now, as a last resort, the status quo sets up a series of traps.

THREE:
SIX TRAPS TO
AVOID ON THE
JOURNEY TOWARD
RADICAL IMPACT

The dragon of the status quo knows that, at its core, the battle for radical impact is a battle between the status quo you and the radical impact you. If you fight your way through the dragon's first line of defenses, then it has a plethora of traps that it knows can kill off your newfound initiative.

The genius of these traps is that they are suggested by the dragon, but set and sprung by you. These are the traps of self-limiting beliefs. There are more self-limiting beliefs in existence than could ever be treated in one book, and they are determined by your upbringing, your life experience, and your own psychological makeup. But over the course of twenty years in the field working with middle managers,

I have observed some beliefs that are particularly common to middle managers. You beat these traps of self-limiting beliefs by becoming aware of them, replacing them with liberating beliefs, and pressing forward through the work of mastery. So let's get to work so that you can get out of your own way and start the hard work toward radical impact.

HARD WORK AND LOYALTY WILL PAY OFF

I was raised by two parents who believed that hard work and loyalty to an employer was the key to career and life success, and for them it was. They worked hard, both of them, and by any societal measure they have been successful. The quintessential middle manager, my father became my early model. His model taught me that if you worked hard for a company and stuck with them, then you would be moved up the ranks over time and would achieve great success.

But the world my father "came up" in did not line up with the world I was living in. His was a baby boomer world driven by the power of American post-war industrial might and a favorable domestic consumer demographic. This was a world of constancy where corporations plodded along and took middle managers along with them for the ride. That was not my world, and it is not yours.

My world and your world, since the early 1990's, has been a digitized world of rapid change, highly competitive, and never the same shape twice. My father's world was a world of American dominance. Now the "world is flat" with emerging economic players all over the world. In this flat world, where anything can be designed, made, and shipped from anywhere in the world to anybody in the world quickly and cheaply, constancy is replaced by chaos.

Radical impact hunters embrace the chaos, and they are not sentimental about the good old days of illusory constancy. Radical impact hunters know that the key to supremacy in this flat world is opportunistic flexibility. Consider the personal risk in picking a company to work for, hoping that they get the "world" right within their context, and that they can keep their mojo working through the multi-decade life span of your career. Add to that the idea that your effort and loyalty, in and of itself, will lead to your advancement and, well, it all sounds rather quaint, doesn't it? And it does not work.

Entire industries emerge and disappear in an instant. If you lived in my home town, North Dallas in the late 90's and early 00's, you witnessed the meteoric rise and then total collapse of the telecom industry (think Nortel), within a ten-year period. If you banked on your career in one of those companies, got hired and parked it, you are lucky to be working as retail store greeter right now. The telecom industry did not care how hard you worked or how loyal you were during that rise and fall. They got it wrong, and when the bottom fell out, so did you. Your hard work and loyalty got you kicked to the curb with the office furniture.

Loyalty to a business should be viewed on a very short-time horizon with an evolving set of exit or launch ramps always in the making. I have seen too many middle managers stay in dead-end jobs in which opportunity for radical impact is limited out of loyalty. I have visited with you after your employer cut you, and you learned the cruel lesson that loyalty was not the two-way proposition you were led to believe. Showing up and chicken-farming or fort-building will not get you anything substantive with anyone you work with or for. Staying in a dead-end job proves nothing about loyalty.

Replace this self-limiting belief with a new liberating belief. The only thing that will guarantee your economic and career stability is the hard work you invest in radical impact creation and the flexibility you apply to its application. Radical impact hunters work hard at creating radical impact and they are, by necessity, nomadic. You must be willing to pack up your tent and move on.

YOU MUST WAIT YOUR TURN

If you are an accountant in a CPA firm or an attorney in a law firm, you work in an "up-or-out" system of advancement with rigid time frames. You know the rules of the game. If you do not advance on schedule through the senior ranks or make partner by a certain number of years, the firm is, in a polite way, telling you to leave. In fact, the advancement, compensation, and profitability of these firms rely on you leaving. For the rest of you, the idea that you must wait your turn to get a promotion or a raise is a self-limiting belief that the status quo business culture imposes to keep you in your place.

An even more destructive variation of the "wait your turn" belief is the belief of "entitled incumbency." This variation goes something like this. Your business knows you should be the person in charge of the department, but the current department head has been there a long time and has done nothing "wrong" per se. When the current department head gets reassigned or retires, it will be your turn to run the department. There is no more stagnating and impact-killing philosophy in a business than the one that advances the belief of entitled incumbency. Business is and should be a "what have you done for me lately" world.

Radical impact hunters do not wait their turn. They put overwhelmingly upward pressure on the organizational chart they work within. They move "up" or they move "out" on their own. Radical impact hunters will not wait for that department head position to open up. They force it open through radical impact. By the sheer impact of the radical impact they create from their position in the business, they expose their chicken-farmer or fort-builder boss as the status quo incremental results people they are. They don't use subtlety, and they don't use politics. Their results are undeniable, significant, and sustainable. They do not give the organization a choice but to let them cut in line. Radical impact hunters have no patience for "entitled incumbency." As an up-and-coming radical impact hunter, you must discard your "wait your turn" mentality, because sometimes the turn never comes. If you are creating radical impact, then you are creating the case for cutting in line and blowing past the sluggish upward mobility of your business' current organizational chart.

YOU ARE DISPENSABLE

In my first week as a manager with General Electric, the director I reported to offered me this little nugget of advice: "The day you are hired here at GE, a bullet is fired with your name on it. Your goal, while here at the company, is to outrun that bullet." The message was loud and clear: "You are easily replaceable. In fact, we are already planning on it. You are dispensable."

If you continue to believe that your value in a business is in showing up, seniority, or loyalty, then you are, indeed, dispensable. If your days are spent chicken farming or fort building, doing rote work that can be automated or outsourced, then your days are numbered. However, if you are an original thinker, with an original voice that transcends the myths of conventional wisdom and structure, and if you combine that originality with unique tactical skills that no one else can deploy or master quickly, then you have changed the calculus in your favor. You have become indispensable.

The liberating belief is to create indispensability. You own your job security and career progression, not your boss.

YOU ARE NOT SMART ENOUGH

Smart is just table stakes for today's middle managers. You must be smart to survive, but brilliance won't necessarily get you much. We are enamored with the genius because we love the outlier. We love the vision of Edison and his light bulb, Einstein and his formula, Picasso and his cubes. But we create a myth around those genius types that limits our own progression in middle management. I have heard it from you over coffee. "Yes, I would love to lead that project, but that is the smart guy stuff. They'll hire a whiz kid for that." Maybe.

But radical impact is within your intelligence set right now. You don't need to be smarter. You need to practice. Some of you will need more practice than others. Nobody is born playing the piano and nobody is innately born with an ability to create sustainable results that matter to a business.

In his book *Outliers,* Malcolm Gladwell reviews the research on mastery that it takes people ten thousand hours of practice to be at an expert level of anything. Geoff Colvin in his book *Talent is Overrated* expands on this idea and exposes the focus and sustained effort such "overnight successes" as The Beatles or "prodigies" like Mozart actually exerted to achieve their success and implied brilliance. Focused and sustained effort will almost always beat innate brilliance (if that even exists).

The key to radical impact creation is not your IQ or where you got your diploma from. It is in your ability to work very hard for a very long time on mastering the technique of creating this radical impact. This is great news. It levels the playing field. It also eliminates competitors. Your potential is not divinely tapped; it is developed. Developing means hard work.

FAILURE IS FATAL

The status quo loves the trap that gets you to believe you that you are judged by how much flawless work you create.

Perfection. Think about that. Where in your life have you ever seen perfection in the physical universe? We live in a physical system that not only falls short of perfection, but relies on it to advance. Evolution happens because of imperfection in genetic codes as they are passed down from generation to generation. Our universe is amassed with variation. Without it, nothing would be exceptional. If the universe didn't have a series of collisions over the millennia, nothing would get created. If nature and the universe require accidents to progress then why do we demand perfection in our businesses? Do we have the hubris to believe we are above it all, not participants in natural and universal law?

Failure is rarely permanent. At its best, failure advances our learning toward radical impact. The key to creating radical impact in business is to continually fail through multiple solutions attempts until you create the radical impact that is sustainable. No business breakthrough of any kind– in revenue, profitability, cash, product, service–occurred dead on right the first time it was tried. And it didn't occur in a lab, on a whiteboard, or in the classroom. It occurred in some portion of the live business. Albert Einstein's notebooks are full of failed formulas as he worked through his theory of relativity. He spent fifteen years failing to describe relativity until he got it right. If Albert Einstein gets to work using trial and error, then so do middle managers creating radical impact.

Replace this self-limiting belief of perfectionism with a new belief that says in order to create radical impact you must make mistakes. You will, should, and must embrace, failing forward. Go break something.

YOU MUST MAINTAIN WORK-LIFE BALANCE

My father-in-law was a veteran of World War II. He was a machine gunner in the Marine Corps and spent the war in the Pacific. He contracted Malaria at Guadalcanal and "hit the beach" at Iwo Jima and Guam. From the time he left Camp Pendleton in California for the Pacific Theatre until he returned home was about three years. He was so emaciated after his tour in the Pacific, as were thousands of other Marines, that the military held these men in quarantine for a month once they got back to the states just so they could fatten them up before they saw their families. He worked his whole career after the war as a sales representative for various products, from "green stamps" to restaurant glassware. And he worked hard. Can you imagine sitting down with him and having a conversation about work-life balance?

The status quo has created the self-limiting belief of work-life balance to keep you from wholly committing to radical impact creation now. The status quo knows that if it can keep you second-guessing yourself and your choices that you will be too distracted to do anything of real value. My father-in-law's view of work was overly stoic. In fact, he told me once that the problem with my generation was that we thought we had to find a job we enjoyed. I understood his position. Compared to the Pacific in World War II, there was no such thing as a bad job. Work-life balance? Heck, he was grateful just to be alive.

I am not telling you to stay in your miserable job. Especially if you become a radical impact hunter, you will have all kinds of career opportunities. What I am telling you is that the path of the radical impact hunter does not take work-life balance into account. Achievement, real achievement, happens when we do what is required rather than what our comfort-seeking self prefers. My father-in-law's example of his service in World War II is extreme to prove a point. He did what millions of his generation did–what was required, not what they preferred.

You are being misled by an onslaught of pop culture entertainers when you are told that you can and must create work-life balance. Instead, aim to create work that integrates with the meaning you have in your life. As a middle manager, you have the opportunity to improve your and your families' lives. You have the opportunity to create jobs and improve other people's lives. You get to bring products and services that the world values to the people who need them. This is valuable work from whatever existential viewpoint you come from. When you integrate your work into your life meaning, then "balance" as an unattainable ideal becomes irrelevant and unnecessary.

As you pursue radical impact, you will miss a kid's soccer game, but you will be a better parent. You may miss a dinner with your significant other, but you will be a better companion. Why? Because the pursuit of radical impact integrates your work with your best self. In the process of becoming a radical impact hunter, you become more human.

READY

Just past sun up, I am lying in the prone position on the grass. My eye is focused on a half-torso silhouette target to my east. To the west, past my feet, is the Pacific Ocean. A slight moist breeze pushes over my back from the water. On the other side of that ocean, Marines paid the ultimate sacrifice in places like Iwo Jima, Korea, and Viet Nam. I am becoming part of the warrior tribe of my father-in-law and his father.

Today is rifle qualification day, a pivotal day in Marine Corps boot camp. Proficiency with a rifle is so ingrained in Marine Corps culture that you are issued your rifle right after you get your "haircut" in boot camp. It goes with you everywhere, and you learn everything there is to know about it. You can assemble and dissemble every component of it in a minute or two. You learn how to clean it and walk with it. And, for two weeks of the thirteen-week boot camp cycle for Marines, you learn to shoot it. You simply cannot be a Marine without demonstrating proficiency with a rifle, and qualification day is the day when every shot counts.

I have shot well, nailing bull's eyes consistently at the two-hundred- and three-hundred-meter mark, racking up points. Now, I begin to fire at the final distance, five-hundred meters, five-and-a-half football fields. It is at this distance that the proficiency of your technique helps you or ruins you, and the number one technique you must have mastered to be a great shot is breath control. *Breathe in, breathe out,* something we do over twenty thousand times a day. But there is a fundamental and critical technique to breathing, firing a rifle, and hitting something on purpose, and I have mastered it. I hit eight of ten bulls eyes at five-hundred meters and qualify as a Marine Corps rifle expert. Prior to joining the Marine Corps, I had never shot a rifle in my life.

This is good news for you as you set out on your transformational journey from chicken farmer and fort builder into radical impact hunter. The difference between where you are now and your radical impact you is commitment and capability. You have set out on the path, with a realistic view of the lay of the land, free from the labyrinth of status quo mythologies, and unencumbered by self-limiting beliefs that trap you in your early steps. Now it is time to master the fundamental technique that will be the sword you wield to kill status quo dragons for the rest of your career.

That sword is strategic execution through the practice of the radical IMPACT cycle.

Let's get started.

RADICAL IMPACT

PART 2:
THE RADICAL
IMPACT CYCLE

FOUR:
INQUIRING

Hemingway kept a journal, Picasso sketched on bistro napkins, and Jimi Hendrix had his guitar slung around his neck everywhere he went so that he could capture riffs when they came to him. Archimedes had his famous "Eureka" moment while sitting in the bath tub. For every great observation, idea, and status quo-busting work that these great creators brought into the world, there were hundreds of ideas that did not get developed, or if they did, they were unsuccessful. To make something spectacular, or discover something new, they have to collect, journal, sketch, riff, doodle, ponder, and soak.

Radical impact hunting is a practice of constant inquiry. This constant state of inquisitiveness engages the creative and the scientific you–the Vitruvian You–in a discovery process that leads to radical breakthroughs. The first victim the status quo dragon captures or destroys in your day-today middle management life is your desire to inquire. It scares you into thinking that inquiry has to do with more work in your lap. So, the first step in your transformation in radical impact hunting is to reengage your inquiry skills. Inquiry needs to be a volume business.

You are, at your core, designed to be inquisitive. Whether you realize it or not, you have already begun the process of inquiring in the first part of this book. By exposing the status quo, you have completed a level of inquiry that most people don't tackle throughout their entire middle management career. It takes a heart of inquiry to ask questions because answers make us accountable. Answers put us on the scent to something greater than where we stand now.

Inquiring starts with a simple exercise that you can do tomorrow morning when you show up to your business for work. The status quo will want you to read through the whole book before trying anything at all. Don't fall for it. Start now.

A SIMPLE SHEET OF PAPER

In the morning, before things get crazy, grab a legal pad, a notebook, or a journal and a pen. Stand up. That's right, stand up. It is time to change your perspective. Write on the top of the sheet of paper today's date and the following phrase: "We could_____if we_____." Radical impact is always a collective achievement. That's why you start the sentence with the word "we." The word "could" opens up a world of possibilities. But we live in the real world where possibilities are always conditional. Conditional on what? That's the "if" in the statement followed up by the conditional of a group "we." What are the possible "coulds?" That's the first blank. What are the conditions that must happen to deliver the coulds? That's the second blank.

The break room chatter in your business is usually not centered around possibilities of achievement. Usually, break room chatter, when focused on business at all, centers around what's wrong with the business, how screwed up the leadership team is, or any number of other gossipy staff rumors that happen to be floating around that day. Break away from that commiserating session today. Make your first move by exploring possibilities from your own point of view: "We could_____if we_____."

Start in your own work area. As you stand there, step outside of your specific job role in your business and look at your job from the outside in as if you were the CEO of the business or a visiting consultant. No one but you will see your list, so let her rip. Be nit-picky. Be unrealistic. Dare and dream. Most of all, be specific.

For example, if you are a buyer or a purchasing manager you might have a "We could_____if we_____" statement that said something such as, "We could *reduce material costs if we bid our commodities more frequently.*" As you progress through your work area, move out into your broader team, your department, your division, and even your business as a whole. Are you a buyer who has a "we could_____if we_____" statement that could improve revenue? Are you a sales manager who has a "we could_____if we_____" statement that could improve shipping accuracy? Are you an accounts receivables manager who has a "we could_____if we_____" statement that could improve a marketing campaign?

Get it out. You are Hemingway, Picasso, and Hendrix–journaling, sketching, and riffing. None of this gets published, shown in the gallery, or put on the album. But you need and own all of it. Keep going until you have at least fifty observations. One hundred would be even better. At this point, you aren't worried about how practical your statements are or how any of them would actually get done. Go for volume. The more statements you have, the more opportunity you will have to get on the scent of radical impact.

How long will it take? If you spend fifteen minutes first thing in the morning for a week, I bet you will have at least fifty. As a consultant, I can come up with fifty "we could_____if we_____" for a business in about an hour, after a few days of observation. But I have practiced this technique for years. This is a new skill for you. Speed is not the objective here; volume is. Pay attention to how you feel as you engage in this step. Notice any tension you experience as you build your "We could_____if we_____" list. Do you feel anxious or nervous as you write down statements about you, your team, or other people's turf? A little anxiety is healthy. It means you have awakened the status quo and made the dragon nervous.

Once you have your list of fifty "We could_____if we_____" statements, congratulate yourself. You have just completed your first level of training in the "Inquiring" phase of the IMPACT cycle. You have broken from the break room crowd and begun the transition to radical impact hunter. You have mimicked the greats in the arts and science. You are Faulkner, Clapton, and Einstein.

Your list acts like an artillery salvo into the camp of status quo dragons in your business. Now that we have awakened the status quo, we need to move swiftly. Pat yourself on the back and then load up your gear. We must move now. The beast is awake and will be on the prowl soon. We must convert these observations into something we can rally support around so that we can take the attack to the enemy.

FIVE: MEASURING

Set your list of "we could____if we_____" statements aside for a moment. Let's discuss the market for your radical impact. That's right, your market. Believe it or not, the great artists and scientists whom everybody knows did not just happen to find their way into your pocket book or textbooks by just being who they were and creating or discovering whatever the wind gave them. Most of them were shrewd marketers or aligned with such people. They saw the progression and trends of their chosen field, believed they could shape the next step, and either developed or already had the technique to execute on the opportunity. After the painting is painted, the book is written, or the song is composed, art is all business. You have heard of the artists and scientists who understand this. You have not heard of the ones who don't. Radical impact hunters celebrate their kills. They parade their quarry through their business and make a big deal about it. You will do the same thing. When you actually create radical impact, you will want to share it within your business context, maybe even your industry as a whole. Why? Because it is a massive middle management achievement to create radical impact, and others will benefit and learn from it. Your ability to create radical impact may provoke others to become radical impact hunters, and you may be part of a new wave of accomplishment in your company. Radical impact is your middle management Mona Lisa or Relativity Theory.

Like the artist and scientist, you must get past people's initial reaction which sounds something like, "So what?"

Enter measuring. What you choose to work on (strategy) must be something that when measured is so mind-blowing that "so what" would only be asked by an uninformed fool in your business (Let's hope that's not the boss.). You will recall that radical impact happens in a business when a middle manager creates a sustainable result that matters. What exactly is a result that matters?

WHAT MATTERS

It doesn't matter if you work in a large, mid-size, or small business. It doesn't matter if you are the CEO or the mail-room clerk. It doesn't matter if you work in sales, operations, marketing, finance, human resources, or IT. You can create a "result that matters" in your business. You can create radical impact.

How do you get past "so what?" By killing that status quo "brush off" with a well-honed and lethal measurement. In the first part of the book, I introduced the five key areas of radical impact. Through mastery of strategic execution you will create radical impact in your business in one of these five results that matter:

GROWING REVENUE

OPTIMIZING PROFITABILITY

CREATING CASH

DIFFERENTIATING CUSTOMER SERVICE

INNOVATING PRODUCT OR SERVICE

Don't let those elephants scare you off. I will cover them in detail in just a minute. Yes, they are massive and substantial. You haven't learned to kill small stuff yet, let alone these colossal beasts. Here are two truths that will keep you from freezing up at this point.

First, every business and every person in every business, including the CEO, struggles with creating radical impact in these five areas. Many business people can create some impact, but it doesn't pass the "So what?" test. And many business people can create a one-time big hit, but that won't pass the sustainability test that is part of the definition of radical impact. Whether you are a shipping manager, a director of sales, a benefits administrator, or the head of accounting, you are in a position to create radical impact in one or all of these five key areas of radical impact.

Second, a result that matters is contextual. This means that if you are working in a multi-billion dollar world-dominating mega-corporation a result that "matters" can pass the "So what?" stage at a relatively small level of absolute value because scale works in your favor. Consider American Airlines CEO Robert Crandall. It had been customary to give first-class passengers an olive with their beverage, but Crandall had noticed that most passengers did not eat their olive. So he eliminated it. When you add up all the first-class passengers on all the flights around the world that American Airlines makes every day, that turns into a lot of olives that don't get bought. It saved the airline about seventy-thousand dollars a year and solidified Crandall as a profit-optimizing zealot. In big companies, olive-sized "So what?" changes can scale to a result that matters very quickly.

In a mid-size or small business, your results that matter will be felt immediately, and they will be noticed. You will still have some opportunities for scaling your victories, and you will have very real opportunity to hit those big five elephants right in the nose. Most mid-size and small business-es have very flat organizational structures. As a result, there is a real chance that as you parade your kill throughout the business the boss will notice and the reward will follow. If you're the boss, then parading your victory throughout a mid-size or small company will drive a radical impact cul-ture into your business.

Here are guidelines for results that "matter" regardless of whether you work in a large, mid-size, or small business.

RADICAL IMPACT MEASUREMENT #1: GROWING REVENUE

Sales leaders and product managers, growing revenue has been and forever will be a target-rich environment for rad-ical impact hunting. When you can grow revenue on pur-pose, you are among the elite radical impact hunters in all of business.

Why? Because growing revenue on purpose is extremely difficult to do.

Recently, I was facilitating a sales strategy session with a mid-size company in the Northeast. Their industry had not recovered from the great recession, and they were strug-gling with growing revenue. The first part of the discussion was driven by the sales leaders themselves. I began with a guiding question designed to provoke discomfort: "How can we grow revenue by 15% this year?" The looks I got were a mix of anger and disbelief. The sales leaders then spent the better part of an hour commiserating on market conditions, the stinginess of their customer base, and the insanity of their competition.

Let's clear this one from the decks right now. One of the tricks of the status quo is to convince you that you are moving heaven and earth just to maintain it. This is a particularly insipid argument made by sales teams. "The market, the customers, the competition is so brutal, we are fortunate just to hold ground," they say.

After the sales leaders vented, we shifted to what we could achieve:

- Were there customers we had sold to that no longer purchased from us?
- Were we pricing our customers correctly so that we maximized our revenue on every sale?
- Were there new customer opportunities that we had a unique advantage to convert?

Once we began breaking the conversation down into executable components, the defensiveness of the status quo began to fade, and real planning began. These sales leaders transformed themselves from sales managers that described failure into middle managers that led radical impact. By the end of the planning session, this group of sales managers had developed an execution plan that would create 10% revenue growth during the year. This plan would not have happened had they not initially framed the discussion with a discomforting break from the status quo.

Where is the radical impact zone in growing revenue? How do you separate normal growth from radical growth? There is no set number. It depends on your specific business context, but let me give you rules of thumb.

If you double the growth rate of your current business or business unit, you are creating radical impact in revenue growth. If your business or business unit is growing at 3% per year, and if you double that to 6% per year, then you have created radical impact. One-hit wonders don't cut it. You must install sustainability into every radical impact effort you undertake. Otherwise, while you might get a parade or promoted, your achievement will be short-lived, and your reputation and future promotion potential will go right along with it.

A double-digit improvement in revenue growth is impressive in nearly every business situation (short of "First mover" contexts). If you can create a 10% or better revenue growth trajectory that is sustainable, then you are creating radical impact. This growth could be in overall revenue or in specific product type sales. It all depends on your level of management and your role in the business. If you are a regional sales manager, then 10% growth in your region is radical impact. If you are product manager, then 10% growth in your product sales across the business is radical impact.

BACK TO THE LIST

Pull out your big list of "We could____if we_____" observational statements. How many of them involve growing revenue? In the margin or on a separate list, designate all of your revenue growth statements. Of your revenue growth statements how many of your "we could"s (the first half of your statements) can be honed into a doubling or 10% growth statement. For example, you might have an initial observation statement that says something such as, "We could grow sales in our Cleveland branch if we improved our quote conversion rate" or "We could sell more light bulbs if we had a more focused marketing effort around selling them." Can you hone these statements in the front half to something such as, "We could grow sales in our Cleveland branch from $10M annual to $11M annual (10% growth) if we improved our quote conversion rate" or "We could improve light bulb sales from $1M annual to $2M annual (doubling) if we had a more focused marketing effort around selling them."

Don't worry about solving anything yet. Determine which observation statements deal with revenue growth and see if you can hone a statement that addresses double-digit growth or doubling revenue. When you have written these statements, set them aside. We will come back to them. By writing these statements, and refining to specificity, you strike a blow to the status quo. You awaken to the idea of possibility. You, like Picasso, or Hemingway or Hendrix have found a path to "the next big thing." You have started to define your middle management magnum opus, radical impact.

RADICAL IMPACT MEASUREMENT #2: OPTIMIZING PROFITABILITY

Beneath the revenue line in every business's income statements are two broad-cost lines that provide an enormous opportunity for radical impact: cost of goods sold and operating costs. Once these two mammoth numbers are subtracted from revenue, the number left over is the operating profit of the business. You will hear this operating profit referred to as net income, EBITDA (earnings before interest, taxes and depreciated assets), or the bottom line. Operating profit is the result of revenue less the cost of the products or services you are selling less the cost of the business to operate. Everything below that operating profit line on income statement concerns the financial structure of the business. While this financial structure of the business is its own specialization with its own opportunity for game-changing impact, we won't try to cover it here. Unless you own the business you are in or are working directly for the board of directors, you are likely not involved with impacting the income statement below the operating profit line. Middle management radical impact opportunity is presented in cost of goods sold reduction and operating expenses reduction.

If you are in operational support functions such as supply chain, distribution, customer service, purchasing, sourcing, or logistics, this is your chance to separate yourself from the status quo pack and make a radical impact. Focus on hard dollar-cost reduction. As a cost manager in your business you would be well served to follow one of my General Electric mentor's points of view on cost. "I don't believe in cost," he would tell me. It wasn't that there was good cost and bad cost. His mindset was that cost shouldn't exist at all. In that world, I had to justify every nickel I spent. I had to convince him that any cost at all was necessary. Consequently, he had the most profitable division in the business.

When you are attacking cost of goods sold, focus on the total cost of product to be available for your use in whatever transformation process you employ. Too many cost of goods sold reduction initiatives focus on unit cost reduction, and by doing so add cost to other areas like payment terms, inbound freight, or large minimum order quantities (which adds inventory holding cost). A good balanced supplier scorecard will make sure you cover all the bases as you attack cost of goods sold.

Operating costs traditionally divide into two groups, fixed costs and variable costs. Fixed costs are things like property, plants, or equipment. Variable costs are any costs tied to your business volume. Like it or not, in most businesses, people costs are variable costs. When you attack variable costs you get the benefit of your business's transactional scale working on your behalf. Your cost savings in variable costs is like an annuity. Every time you send out an order to a customer, the business benefits. Robert Crandall understood the power of variable-cost reduction when he got rid of that olive.

Whether you are working on cost of goods sold reduction, fixed cost reduction, or variable cost reduction, focus on cost reductions that don't require other costs to achieve the reduction, like expensive software or consultants. Then, you have to learn to communicate your wins in a language most businesses understand. The sad fact of the matter is that operational types dramatically under-report their operating profit impact. Their impact is drowned out by the revenue hounds in the business. As a result, they don't get the radical impact credit they deserve.

Cost hunters, you have to learn to communicate your wins in radical terms so that you get credit for your hard-won victories against the status quo. This is not "spin" or "perception" management. This is real deal communications that demonstrate clearly and in no uncertain terms your radical impact on operating profit improvement. Let me show you two ways to tell the story of your achievement that really bring home the radical IMPACT of your cost work.

COVER YOUR/YOUR TEAM COST FIRST

This radical impact play was a play I used twice in GE, and it resulted in two promotions in three years and a thirty-five percent increase in personal income. It is a great play if you work in a traditional "cost center."

Here's how it works. Let's say you have a team of three people, yourself and two others. You draw an annual salary of sixty thousand dollars per year, and your team members draw a salary of fifty thousand dollars per year each. Your team costs the business $160,000 of salary per year. When you add the cost of typical employment taxes and benefits cost that the business carries on your behalf, the real "fully loaded" cost of compensation and benefits for your team will land somewhere around $210K per year. If you are not in a revenue-producing group, you are a cost center, a necessary group for the business to operate with stability. I led a sourcing team at GE. We produced no revenue. We only spent money. How could I get the parade with a radical impact kill while producing no revenue?

My team and I decided that we would cover our cost and even create an implied return on the investment of our cost by tackling one of the big five of the radical impact opportunities, optimizing profitability. We went on a mission to reduce the cost of the products we sourced. By reducing the cost of the products we sourced, without reducing the price we charged for those products, we would improve the gross margin dollars coming into our business unit. By improving gross margin dollars without adding any more cost to make that improvement, all of our gross margin improvement would "fall" to the bottom line and improve the operating profitability of our business unit. The $210K annual cost I showed was not the cost of the team I led. In fact, the cost of that team was significantly higher. But let's stay with this $210K number for now.

We decided that since the gross margin of our business unit was about 20% that we would provide enough product cost deflation through our team's effort to cover our team's cost plus a 20% implied return to the company. So, we needed to create about $260K worth of cost reduction to accomplish a result that mattered to our business unit. We did. In fact, we doubled our target, and we were not quiet about it.

Everyone on that team got raises, some got stock options, and one got promoted. What we accomplished and paraded around the business had not been done before. The idea of a self-funded cost center was a radical solution to create a radical impact. It is still a great tactic for those of you in non-revenue producing functions.

EXPRESS YOUR IMPACT IN SALES-EQUIVALENT DOLLARS

Another effective way to measure impact that matters when your role involves optimizing profitability is to express your impact in sales-equivalent dollars.

Here's how it works. Let's say you are the operations manager of a $50M company. That company has a 10% return on sales. It takes $50M worth of revenue every year for this company to create $5M worth of operating profit. Through your mastery of strategic execution, you have created a shipping process that saves your business $100K of hard-dollar freight expense. If you express the fruits of your effort as a simple cost reduction you might get a high five, but no parade.

We have not expressed the achievement in one of the five key areas of radical impact. The bosses don't care about cost-cutting. They care about optimizing profitability. To create a result that matters, we have to express the result in a terminology that matters. When you reduce cost by $100K a year without having to spend money to do it, you create hard-cost efficiency. For a $50M business with a 10% bottom line to produce $100K of additional operating margin through the sales side of the business, they would have to produce $1M worth of new sales without adding any additional costs. That means $1M of new sales without any additional sales people, marketing people, inventory, locations, promotional literature, and customer dinners, none of it. You did not create $100K of hard freight cost reduction in your business. You improved profitability $100K with a sales equivalency of $1M. That impact gets a parade.

When you express your results in a language that resonates with the five key areas of radical impact you leverage your results into the language of radical impact.

BACK TO THE LIST

Pull out your big list of "We could____if we_____" observational statements. How many of them involve improving operating profit by reducing cost of goods sold, fixed cost, or variable cost? In the margin or on a separate list, designate all of your operating profit improvement statements. Of your operating profit improvement statements, how many of your "we could"s (the first half of your statements) can be honed into a "pay-for-yourself statement?" For example, you might have an in initial observation statement that says something like this, "We could save $100K per year on our purchases of tooling if we strategically sourced our tooling and moved our purchases to the least total cost supplier." Convert that statement into a sales equivalent dollars statement: "A $100K annual savings on tooling purchases would be the equivalent of $2M in annual sales growth (assuming a 5% bottom line). We could create the equivalent of $2M in annual sales growth if we strategically sourced our tooling and moved our purchase to the least total cost supplier." That statement will wake up everybody in the business, including the dragon.

Just as before, when you have these statements written out, set them aside. We will come back to them.

RADICAL IMPACT MEASUREMENT #3: CREATING CASH

I worked at GE during a time of great prosperity in the company. As GE exited the twentieth century, Jack Welch had converted a stodgy appliance manufacturing business into an international colossus of wide-ranging manufacturing, services, and financial management instruments. One of Jack Welch's mantra's was "Cash is king." GE had billions of dollars of cash on its balance sheet. Some investment analysts criticized GE for holding on to too much cash, but

Welch did not waver in his commitment to cash conservation and creation. As the twentieth century came to a close and saw rise to the dot com boom, GE's commitment to cash paid off. Valuations of businesses with unsupported balance sheets that subsequently collapsed (think Enron) made GE's stodgy commitment to cash seem, well, enlightened, and the stock price reaped the rewards.

There is a great untapped potential for radical impact in most businesses. Cash creation links to revenue, net income, and asset utilization, and those managers who can master it can differentiate themselves from the chicken farmers and fort builders. Cash creation is both an opportunity for you to create radical impact and another way for you to express your achievements as a middle manager in a clear and impactful way.

Cash is created in a business when the cash used to fund payables, receivables, and inventory is less than the cash created by the business operating income. Cash is drained in a business when the cash used to fund payables, receivables, and inventory is greater than the cash created by the business operating income. The common measurement for most of us in business to use to express this relationship is "Cash Flow from Operating Activities," or CFOA. Cash is used for other things in the business financial structure, and ultimately this business financing structure impacts the total cash available in any business. But, just as in operating profit, we want to focus our effort on those areas of the business we can radically impact. Most of us can impact a business's operating profit, and most of us can impact a business's "cash flow from operating activities."

When you improve operating profit without having to pay suppliers more quickly, collect money from customers more slowly, or increase inventory investment, you create cash. Just as you can express your operating profit wins in sales equivalent dollars, you can also express them in their impact to cash.

Remember how we expressed your big win in tooling cost reduction, as "A $100K annual savings on tooling purchases would be the equivalent of $2M in annual sales growth (assuming a 5% bottom line)"? We could create the equivalent of $2M in annual sales growth if we strategically sourced our tooling and moved our purchase to the least total cost supplier." We can beef that statement up with a cash statement: "A $100K annual savings on tooling purchases would be the equivalent of $2M in annual sales growth. This savings would not negatively impact payables, receivables, or inventory. So this $100K of annual savings would improve cash by $100K." Who would not want to sign up to help with this radical impact initiative?

As you robustly communicate and think through the radical impact opportunity of your observations, you begin to change the way your ideas are expressed. Your vocabulary is amped up to a radical level. You aren't just making passing comments to the boss in the hall, hoping for a pat on the back. You are stating real business radical impact potential, and it will get noticed.

Lots of you can have radical impact in cash creation. If you are in an accounts payable group, you can look for ways to negotiate more favorable and longer payment terms with suppliers. If you are in credit, collections, or any other group that is touching accounts receivable functions, you can free up cash by getting money from customers more quickly. Here, also, there is a balance. Companies that are too tight on credit or too aggressive on late invoice collections can often, inadvertently, restrict growth.

If you are in the world of inventory management, you have the opportunity to free up cash by using less inventory to service customers, distribution centers, or manufacturing facilities. Any time you can reduce inventory in relation to operating profit, you free up cash. The balance here is that you have to maintain enough inventory to service customers, distribution, and manufacturing facilities.

Pull out your big list of "We could____if we_____" observational statements. How many of them involve freeing up cash by actions in accounts payable, accounts receivable, or inventory? In the margin or on a separate list, designate all of your cash creation statements. Of your cash creation statements, how many of your "we could"s (the first half of your statements) can be honed into a "pay for yourself/ or your department statement"? Convert your statements to cash impact as in the examples shown. Again, don't try to figure out how you will create the cash you have identified. Instead, go through your observation statements that deal with cash creation and see if you can create "pay for yourself/your team" and articulate that statement in cash creation. Now, you are developing a big list of opportunities to have impact in revenue, operating profit, and cash creation. Think of your business in terms of its financial statements. In these three groups of observations, you are impacting the income statement (revenue and operating profit), the cash flow statement (cash flow from operating activities), and the balance sheet (asset efficiency in the form of cash). You have hit all the big stuff right in the mouth.

RADICAL IMPACT MEASUREMENT #4: DIFFERENTIATING CUSTOMER SERVICE

You have been in this meeting dozens of times throughout your middle management work life. It may be at the tail end of the Thanksgiving potluck or at some quiet moment in the annual kickoff meeting, but you have been there. The head of the business, division, or location stands up, sometimes grabs the microphone, and says something such as, "I just want to take a moment and recognize some of our people who do such an outstanding job taking care of our customers. Why just yesterday I received an email from a customer that I would like to share." Then the boss reads the email that sings the praises of the business's outstanding customer service ethic. And this is a great thing. Bosses should call out team members who are being praised by customers. But what you would like to see is a customer service level so differentiated and radical that the boss's email is flooded with customer praise, and there wouldn't be enough time in the day for her to single out everyone who is mentioned by happy customers.

Is that your business? Are you overwhelmed with customer satisfaction? Or do you get read the one email the boss got before the potluck?

There is a dramatic opportunity to create radical impact by innovating customer service differentiators in your business. It is a paradox in the age of connectivity that we live in now that while answers for nearly everything concerning our transactions with a business are at our finger tips, our perception of customer service is that it has eroded or disappeared altogether. Why is that? I believe it is because we have confused access to information with customer service and that we have made the assumption that people really want to self-serve everything. You print your own boarding passes for airlines, you check yourself out at the grocery store, and you hit button after button on your cell phone as you navigate the labyrinth of automated decision trees when you call a company, any company, to ask a question. All of these self-service functions have stripped out cost for the providers and stripped out time for those of us who use them. On the face of it, these cost-saving and time-saving innovations seem great. But what they have done, in reality, is commoditized the customer service opportunity that a transaction creates.

You would be hard-pressed to create a business case that could prove out that the number one best path to revenue growth is anything other than retaining the customers you have and sell them more stuff more often. The cost of acquiring new customers is really that high. Yet, our service mentality, whether it be in business to consumer or business-to-business, has taken the attitude that existing customers need to be serviced with the least amount of our time as possible. Automated technology that delivers customers with efficient DIY answers is not differentiating customer service. Personable service matters.

How do you measure the impact of service differentiation? Customer surveys are intrusive and have a miserable response rate. Waiting on "you're awesome" emails is too anecdotal to base your career progression on them. You need a system of measurement inside your business that can gauge the satisfaction of your customers that differentiated service can provide.

Logistically, the gold standard for customer satisfaction is a measurement called the "perfect order" score. This measurement looks at three basic components of customer service:

1. **Did the customer get the order on time?** That means the customer received the order when he wanted to receive it, not when we could get it to him.

2. **Did the customer get the order in full?** That means that everything the customer ordered was in the box, not some of it, not most of it, but all of it.

3. **Did the customer get the order error-free?** That means no mistakes on what we shipped, how we shipped, the condition we shipped in, and the accuracy of our pricing. Simply, no mistakes.

You will hear this metric referred to as OTIFEF (On Time, In Full, Error Free). It is a tough metric to hit for many companies. Most mid-market companies I have worked with aren't even measuring it when I first show up. When I ask them how they differentiate themselves logistically, I usually get one of two answers: "Our customers love us" or "We work hard to take care of our customers." Both of these statements may or may not be true, but without a systematic approach to logistical differentiation your customer service impact is either bad, hidden, or nothing special.

If you work in or touch the logistics function in your business, you have a clear path to radical impact here. Improving on time delivery, order fill rates, or order accuracy to drive up your perfect order score is a proven differentiator of customer service. You will retain customers when you have differentiating levels of perfect order scores compared to your competition.

Customer touch is a differentiator understood more in the business-to-consumer business rather than in the business-to-business world, but both modes of customer service offer opportunity to create radical impact. If part of your business role involves direct customer interaction, think through all the points of contact with your customer bases in which you could "de-commoditize" the experience and differentiate. You may discover that you can differentiate in a number of areas: from the way you communicate product or technical knowledge to the way you quote complex requests, from your response time to requests for help to your proactive reporting of things your customer cares about, from custom service programs to expediting information delivery, from return policies to billing accuracy. In each of these areas, you can change the status quo game and make a significant difference in your customer's interaction with your business.

The big measurement here is customer retention. If you differentiate your service, you will retain more customers than you will with commoditized customer service. Even a 10% improvement in customer retention will have radical impact on the revenue line of your business. Become different, become great, and keep those customers you worked so hard to gain in the first place.

Try this simple action. Pull out your big list of "We could____if we_____" observational statements. How many of them involve differentiating customer service through logistics impact or customer touch impact? In the margin or on a separate list, designate all of your customer service observations.

RADICAL IMPACT MEASUREMENT #5: INNOVATING PRODUCT OR SERVICE

New products, new ways to sell existing products, or new services to offer that enhance your current offering are not topics limited to research and development teams or the marketing department. Anyone in any business at any time can come up with a radically new product or service to sell to existing and new customers.

Measuring radical impact here is relatively straightforward. Did the new product or service you created result in new revenue from existing customers or new revenue from new customers? If either of these results exist in a significant quantity, then you are creating radical impact through product or service innovation, and anyone can innovate.

BACK TO THE LIST

Go through your list one more time. Are any of your "We could_____if we_____" statements centered around new product or service innovation? "Sticky notes" were a new product innovation that an engineer at 3M developed in his free time. Howard Schultz did not invent the cup of coffee. He innovated the way people experienced the cup of coffee. Make notes in the margin or create a new list for all the product or service innovations you have gathered in your observations. Will this product or service innovation improve revenue by more than 10%? Will this product or service innovation double revenue in a location, product team, division, or business? If the answer to either of these questions is yes, then you may be onto something.

What you have now is a honed list from your original list of observations. You have also performed the "thought" work to express your "We could_____if we_____" portion of your statements into assertions of hard measurable, specific, radical impact. You have value statements related to growing revenue that demonstrate the possibility of double-digit growth or even doubling of current revenue. You have statements related to optimizing profitability that pay for yourself or your team. You have statements for creating cash that improve cash flow from operations. You have statements to differentiate service that will improve perfect-order scores or customer retention.

You also have thought like an innovator and created statements around product or service innovation that will improve revenue with existing customers or create an entirely new customer base.

You may have "We could_____if we_____" statements in all of these areas of impact, or you may have stayed within your area of functional expertise. Either way, you have laid out one or a series of radical impact opportunities for your business. At this point, you have gone as far as you can go alone. Now, it is time to use these defined possibilities to rally support. You can't kill the dragon of the status quo by yourself, and you will have to make a hell of pitch to get help doing it. So let's go get your posse.

SIX:
PROTOTYPING

Now that you have qualified your observations and completed your intelligence-gathering, it is time to test solutions in your live business. Let's gather a team, prioritize our targets of opportunity, develop a minimal viable plan, and test our solution with live ammo. That will wake up some people. It's time to prototype.

Prototyping is a necessary stage that involves your testing out your plan before actually executing it into full-blown action. Prototyping will feel uncomfortable for most of you. At this stage of your training you will be tempted to take a deep analytical dive into all the possible paths toward improvement. You will want to study, plan, and plan some more. You will want to fall into the trap of the perfect answer. And it is just that, a trap of the status quo that feeds off of the myth that you should not fail.

Press forward and fend off that voice in your head that says, "You don't know what you are doing." The truth is, you *don't* know what you are doing, not yet anyway. And you won't know what you are doing until you actually *do* it. Train with live ammo. Plan just enough in the prototype stage so that you don't shoot yourself in the foot, but don't plan enough to make yourself comfortable. Over-planning is for amateurs, and it creates the illusion that real work is being done. I'll take one sloppy doer to ten precise planners any day of the week. The real radical impact hunters plan just enough to move and then lace up their boots and go kick ass.

TEAMS WIN

The team I was on at a mid-market industrial distributor had been preparing for the big "pitch" for over a month. We worked nights, weekends, ate lunch at our desks, ate dinner at our desks, slept at our desks, and we were ready. We were ready to pitch a status quo-busting business proposal that, if accepted, would double the size of our company nearly overnight, transform us into a regional powerhouse, and positively impact all of our careers.

Think about the company you hire to fix a circuit breaker at your house or run a new electric service to part of your business facility. More than likely you hire an electrical contractor to do that. Now, think about the company you hire to design the electrical system for a baseball stadium or a wafer fabrication plant. You would hire an electrical engineering firm to do that. When you combine an electrical contractor firm with an engineering firm, you had our customer, a monster consumer of the products we sold as an electrical distributor. These guys could wire up your pool pump or wire up a seventy-story building.

As big as they were, they purchased their electrical products the same way everybody else did, status quo. They would prepare lists of material that they needed, send the list to us and to about half a dozen of our competitors, receive the bids back, evaluate all of them, and reward a purchase order to the low bidder (usually). It was a clunky process that took a lot of manpower and time, and we were out to change all of that.

We formed a sales team comprised of outside and inside sales people, project managers and operational managers, all familiar with this customer's business. Initially, we wanted to answer a selfish question, "How could we improve our win percentage on the bid requests we were receiving from this customer?" By answering that question we covered familiar ground and were moving right along traditional answers where the status quo wanted us to go. The status quo loves sending you down the "me too" solution path. It throws you off the scent.

At some point in our deliberation, someone asked the question, "What if we could eliminate the bid process with this customer altogether?" The beauty of that team of people is that everyone thinks they were the one who asked that pivotal question. Everyone on that team wanted to contribute at a high level. Regardless of who asked the question, the question of eliminating a decades' old bid process became the rallying point for a month-long preparation and ground-laying effort.

The outside sales team probed and tested lines of rationale with key decision makers inside the customer. The inside sales team and project managers probed field members of the customer and dialed into the idea of a single provider. The operations team calculated the logistical cost savings both companies could generate if we contracted in a blanket purchase arrangement. Every cost was accounted for, and a win/win financial proposition presented itself. Each of us pitched our part of the program to the board of our customer, a blanket purchasing agreement that would eliminate bidding out shopping lists to the market as a whole. Our pitch was thorough, detailed, unified, and successful. We were awarded the business, and it doubled the size of our company. It was a true team win. Every member's contribution was critical, and without total commitment and effort the outcome would have been different. We changed the way an industry operated and were rewarded for the change. But we centered on the question, were determined to kill the dragon of the status quo, and blew it away.

GET A TEAM

The key to transitioning from a smart person with a list of honed "We could_____if we_____" statements to radical impact is collaboration. You need help. You need lots of solution ideas, more than you can possibly come up with on your own. You need to work like great artists and scientists have worked over the ages.

We have a stereotypical idea of the uber-brilliant, as a loners living out by the pond, madly working through every idea with frenetic and fanatical energy. It is a myth advanced by the status quo to scare you out of being creative. Who wants to be the crazy person in the woods? The mad genius? I don't and neither have most real artists and scientists. T.S. Eliot, arguably the greatest poet of the twentieth century, relied heavily on his collaboration with Ezra Pound in order to produce the master works he is known for. Picasso, perhaps the greatest painter of the twentieth century, discovered "Cubism" in a collaborative effort with another great but lesser known painter of the era, Georges

Braque. Wernher von Braun led a team of scientists and engineers to get men on the moon through the American Apollo program. Creatives like Eliot, Picasso, and von Braun were comfortable with the limits of their own perception and idea sets. The genius in their creativity was in their ability to take input and collaboration with various sources and consolidate that input and collaboration into something new, unique, substantial, radical.

You have Pounds, Braques, and von Braun's team in your business right now. They might be waiting on you to ask them to jump in and solve the tough stuff. Ask them. You don't have to create a "what's in it for them" proposition. There are people in your business who want to create radical impact but don't have a vehicle in which to create it. They want to achieve great things but can't get out of the fort or off the farm. What's in it for them is the same thing that is in it for you—impact, achievement and meaning, I AM. Go and hunt them, regardless of their job function, title, or department. In fact, the more cross-functional your team, the better. You need a team of three or five. There will be votes, so you want that odd number. Don't start with a team greater than five. It will be unwieldy. Remember, you are practicing right now. Do not wait on permission to form your team. Identify whom you want and "pitch" them your series of honed "We could_____" statements. Take them to lunch. Go through your list. Ask them point blank, "Wouldn't you like to be on a team that makes a significant and sustainable impact in this business?" You will get takers. Take them. Will you step on toes? Maybe. But I have yet to see a boss who would tell you to stop. They might ask you some questions about what you are doing, what you are up to. They may want to be sure that your day-to-day duties will not suffer. After all, they have their own forts and farms to run. But they will not tell you to stop.

You are a leader when you decide to be. You lead when people agree to be led by you. If they join in your effort, they have made the agreement. You are now leading a renegade band of dragon-killers. You have gathered in the "small" conference room of your building. You have a team, a list, and no clue what to do next. Let's start by cutting down your list.

PRIORITIZE TARGETS OF OPPORTUNITY

Remember, strategic execution is deciding what to work on and how to do it. Prioritizing is the first step in the strategic portion of strategic execution. We need to decide what this team is going to undertake, and that starts with prioritization. You have already entered the land beyond the maps. You are not the first band of marauders who have attempted to hunt down the dragon of the status quo. Many, many have been lost in the effort. Most are lost right out of the gate. They can't decide what to commit to, what to work on, where to focus their energies. They take on a little bit of everything and dive into planning. They can't win the fight because they never get to the fight.

Everything on your honed list of "We could_____if we_____" statements is an opportunity for radical impact. The temptation of your team at this point will be to try to tackle too much. You can fight and defeat exactly one status quo dragon at a time right now. If you try to take on more than one, you either won't find them, or you won't beat them. The effort and act of prioritizing allows you and your team to find that one faint drift of smoke on the horizon, deliberately march to it, and obliterate it in its sleep.

Strategy is as much about saying "no" as it is anything else. The trick is to eliminate the ones that can wait, have less impact than you originally thought, or may be too powerful at this time for you to overcome. Prioritization allows you to decide where to exert sustained and focused effort. T.S. Eliot abandoned his PhD work to focus on writing. Pablo Picasso shrugged off his formal training in Spain to focus on new painting forms in Paris. Wernher von Braun focused his time on one rock in an infinite universe, the moon. They all focused obsessively and collaborated with like-minded peers, just like you will.

Gather your team for your first strategy session. Meet in a small break-out room, conference room, or your living room–somewhere out of the line of fire from the day-to-day. Then follow this simple game plan.

1. On a white board or big sheet of paper draw the following four-block grid:

2. Provide each of your team members a list of your honed "We could_____if we_____" statements. It is still not time to spend any effort on the back half of that statement, "if we_____." You and your team will now give each of your statements a score based on how they would place on the four block grid.

3. Then raise these questions: How much impact will one opportunity have over the other opportunities in the list? How difficult will it be to achieve that opportunity versus the difficulty in achieving that opportunity with other observations?

4. Then rate each one on a simple scale of 1-4.

If you have an observational statement that would create a high level of impact and would not be terribly difficult to implement, then you would give it a score of "1." If you have an observational statement that would create a high level of impact and would be fairly difficult to implement, then you would give it a score of "2." If you have an observational statement that would create a lower level of impact but would be fairly easy to implement, then you would give it a score of "3." Finally, if you have an observational statement that would create a lower level of impact and would be fairly difficult to implement, then you would give it a score of "4."

What makes something easy or difficult to implement? Opportunities have a low degree of implementation difficulty when they have some readily available measurement system in place, can be solved with a few empowered people, and can use existing technology systems in place in the business right now. Opportunities get difficult to realize with implemented solutions when they have no easy or readily available measurement system in place in the business, require a significant amount of cross-functional cooperation, or need massive technology investment to make it all work.

You and your team will have differing points of view, and that difference is exactly what you want. Your initial impact statements may be overstated or understated. Your team will let you know. You need a range of viewpoints when you are tackling the "difficulty" question. What you may see as a simple path may be very complicated to a team member. Here is the place for discussion and debate.

It is important that you arrive at consensus for your scoring at this point. Without consensus here, you are already sowing the seeds of division and dissension, and you won't sustain the impeding attacks from the status quo if you, as a team, are not in complete, blood oath agreement. Do not leave this ranking exercise until you have hammered out consensus. This may take you and your team an hour. It may take you a day. Take what it takes. Consensus rules at this point.

Once you have a consensus score on each of your opportunity statements, eliminate the "2's," "3's," and "4's." Shove them aside, put them in a folder, store them in the cloud, but get them out of your way. You might come back to these at a later date. You might reevaluate them down the road. But for now, they are goners. If you have more than one opportunity statement that is getting a score of "1," put a fresh four-block grid back up on the board or on a new sheet of paper and run your number "1's" through the evaluation cycle again.

Your goal is to end up with one opportunity statement that rises above all the others and that the team has one hundred percent consensus on. This is the one single most important decision you will make that will determine whether or not you have a fighting chance against the status quo. Arrive at a single consensus opportunity statement and you have a chance. Fail to reach consensus or fail to commit to one opportunity statement, and you might as well pack the tent and go apologize to everyone for burning down the fort and the farm. It is that critical that you either leave the room, arms locked, ready for the next step, or go your separate ways. I am guessing you are ready to fight.

MAP

You have the same creative capacity as every great master of every art form and every discoverer of every great scientific advance ever in the history of the human race. You were born with "Vitruvian" DNA. It's time you and your team started using that capacity.

Armed with team consensus and with focus on one opportunity, it is time to begin connecting the opportunity of the thing, with the execution of the thing. Remember, planning will be minimal at this point because what we are driving to right now is to get to a prototype, a small experiment, that we can try out in the live business that will prove out the method for our full assault on the status quo. For this first part, think of yourself as the artist sketching, jotting, and riffing around a central idea, your opportunity or the scientist tinkering in the lab. The game at this point is quantity of ideas not quality. No one will see this except you and your team. It will be sloppy and daring, maybe even a little crazy or bizarre, but be that awesome and fearless.

Gather your team for another strategy session. Have on hand a clean whiteboard or a sheet of paper. Now we go to work on the other half of your "We could_____if we_____" statement. In the center of the whiteboard or on your sheet of paper, write your "We could_____" statement. From our earlier example it might say, "We could improve light bulb sales from $1M to $2M annual." Next, above, below, and to each side of that statement write the word, "If." Now, fill in your first "if" statement, the one you came up with in your very early initial observation. Your initial "if" statement was this: "if we had a more focused marketing effort around selling them."

With your opportunity illustrated in the middle of this white space surrounded by conditions, "ifs," and your one condition, it is time to engage the team. First, gather all the big "if" statements. What can they add? How many other "ifs" can you come up with? The whole page is available to list as many "if" statements as possible. Some "if" statements will lead to other "if" statements. Draw lines connecting them. Make a mess. You are done when you have filled up the page or run out of "if" statements. I have seen teams complete this iteration in thirty minutes of idea-flying heat, and I have seen it take several hours. However long it takes, teams generate dozens of paths to achieve the opportunity.

Just as you can't hunt down more than one radical impact opportunity at a time, when you are just learning the skill, you can't prototype more than one "if" statement at a time. The purpose of the mapping exercise you just completed was to generate a lot of options. Prolific option generation is key to solving impact opportunities. What you will witness in your "if" mapping iteration is many "if" statements coming from your team members that you had not thought of. That's the first power of teams. You need every idea you can get because at this point you are not sure which one will work.

Now you're ready to pursue the next question: "Which path do we take?" Return to the prioritiziation matrix, and rank your "if" statements in the same rigor as you ranked your "We could_____" honed opportunity statements. As you rank your "if" statements, you home in on your execution plan. The "if" statements are identifying a gap, something to be attacked. Picking the "if" to attack is also a strategic decision, but it moves you toward the "how" of execution. Your goal in this ranking iteration is to find the "if" statements that score the number "1."

Just like the ranking iteration of the "We could_____" statements, identify "if" statements that could drive the maximum impact toward your radical impact opportunity with the least amount of difficulty to implement. You may have several "if" statements that score as a "1." Again, do the work as a team to narrow and get consensus on a single "if" statement.

You may be asking, "But what if the 'if' statement we settle on won't get us all the way toward our radical impact opportunity?" It won't. The radical impact opportunity you have identified is massive. It is a five-hundred-ton dragon. It is boiling the ocean and solving world hunger all at the same time. No single "if" statement on your board will accomplish that. It may take execution of three or four "if" statements to realize your radical impact. It may take execution of every single one of them, plus twenty more you haven't thought of yet. It all depends on how complex the path is to your impact.

This is a dangerous point in your training. This is where the yellow brick road, that seems so cool in the first few steps, disappears into infinity. This is where you get overwhelmed by the status quo. That overwhelmed feeling you have in your gut means you are on the verge of something radical. It means you have joined the ranks of business creatives who, like you, have sat staring at a board full of "ifs" and felt the same pang. The status quo is wrong, of course. You will solve this. Let me show how you.

THE LAW OF GRADUALISM

The first job I had after my hitch in the Marine Corps was for a company that modified military aircraft for different types of military missions. I had been an aircraft electrician in the Marines, so the job was right up my alley. I was hired to install forward-looking infrared systems and terrain following radar on C-130 aircraft. My first day on the job, the foreman took me up to the aircraft I was assigned to and gave me my first assignment: wire up a terminal board. Eager to show that they had hired the right guy, I took my blue prints, flashlight, and tools, and then wedged myself into the space.

Picture a ball that is about as wide as the top of your desk and about three feet tall. Now picture that the ball is made up of individual wires about half the width of a standard issue office ink pen. It would take thousands of wires to make up a ball this size. That's what met me in the crawl space underneath the pilot's seat, a giant nest of wires and a blank terminal board. For what seemed like hours I stared at the ball and at my blueprints and back to the ball, then back to the blueprints. I played a movie in my mind of day after day crawling into this space and making order out of the chaos in front of me. This job was going to take a long time. So was going to college at night, raising a family, and building a career, by the way.

I knew I couldn't sit there and stare. I wasn't being paid to be dumbfounded. I was being paid to wire up a terminal board. So, I devised a clever method to get the ball in order and get the job done. Get ready to have your doors blown off with this clever and innovative method. I took the first wire I could get a hold of, looked it up on the drawing to find which terminal it went to, then I hooked it up to that terminal. Then, I took the next wire I could get a hold of, looked it up on the drawing to find which terminal it went to, then I hooked that wire up to the appropriate terminal. Then, I repeated these steps about four thousand times until the job was complete.

Most complicated, overwhelming tasks get solved one way: "One wire at a time." It's not hard. It just takes commitment and faith that with each painstakingly gradual step you take, you get one step closer to achieving the task. With each word that is written, the book gets closer to realization, with each brush stroke applied to the canvas, the painting comes into view, and with each "if" statement completed radical impact gets closer to realization and the blade is sharpened.

This is the law of gradualism, and there is no shortcut to it. You must walk into oblivion. You must embrace the overwhelming nature of what you are taking on. And then you must break it down into its smallest executable units and put your radical impact opportunity together one wire at a time. Your smallest executable unit, right now, is the "if" statements you have on the board. They are your tangled ball of wire. Pick one, based on the ranking rigor (your blueprint), and let's get to work on it. There is no time to lose.

Now we make a rapid shift out of strategy and into execution mode. You now have a statement that says something like this: "We could improve light bulb sales from $1M annual to $2M annual if we had a more focused marketing effort around selling them." Since this statement is addressing only one of the possible "ifs" in your initial evaluation, we can rewrite it to accept the fact that this is a first step:

"We have identified an opportunity for radical impact in our business. We believe that we can begin the process of improving light bulb sales from our status quo performance of $1M annual sales to a $2M annual sales. There are several initiatives that we will need to undertake to achieve this radical impact. After an initial evaluation, we will be working on developing a more focused marketing effort. We believe this improvement, above all other possible improvement efforts we have identified will deliver the earliest and most substantial impact toward our potential, and will be the easiest improvement to implement."

You now have a clear strategic mission. That is your first real blow to the status quo! Armed with that and the resilience to embrace the law of gradualism you are ready to shift into full execution mode of your prototype solution.

MINIMAL AND VIABLE

You and your team have completed mind mapping and have a clear mission statement to deliver radical impact. In the light bulb illustration you would have several notes or bullet points under the action "developing a more focused marketing effort." Next, refine that statement and build a small experiment that you can test out in your live business. The reality is that most businesses exit any kind of strategic planning session with a statement like the one we presented in the previous section. Many planners can arrive at a goal and at an initial approach to achieve that goal.

What's so hard about that? Nothing. Strategy is simple. Do a little homework, get in a room, come up with consensus, and eliminate everything else. Yet, this is where most business initiatives come to a grinding halt. Why? Because while strategy is relatively simple, execution is challenging. When you are executing a strategic decision, you come up against everything the status quo has to throw at you. That dragon will let you sit in that conference room all day long and strategize. It knows that as long as you never get out of the talking phase of a radical impact idea, you are harmless. You get the dragon's attention as soon as you leave that conference room with steps toward execution of the strategy. Now, and only now, you are dangerous in the mind of the dragon. If you are not crafty, you will walk into the dragon's first trap. Many radical impact strategies fail in early execution because they try to solve too much. They get shot down as too risky by those in charge, or, even if allowed to get some traction, they are abandoned at the first sight of trouble. We must be more clever than that when implementing our strategy. We can flank the status quo with a simple tactic, starting small. Artists and scientists use this tactic, and we can copy it. We need a rough draft, a sketch, a lick, a small experiment that we can try out in a small critique group or club downtown, before we hit up the major publishers, galleries, performance venues, or research institutes.

So, we start small. And when we have worked out the kinks and our radical impact execution solution is ready for prime time, we roll it out to the broader business. Jack

Welch, the former CEO of GE, used to call these tests "cheap experiments." They were cheap both in cost and in risk, and it is a very effective tactic for sneaking up on a dragon. The execution example that we are using states that in order to achieve our radical revenue improvement target we need to "develop a more focused marketing effort." We need to break that statement down into three areas of change that we can test out in a small location, department, or market.

What specific steps can we take that will create a "more focused marketing effort?" Do we need a procedure, a work flow, or a checklist? Do we need a decision tree or prioritization exercise to focus our marketing effort?

Affecting change means changing how work is done. If we don't change a process, we won't change outcomes. It is a fundamental truism and a law of nature in business. But think about that for a minute. One of the reasons so many strategies don't get past the talking stage is that we don't ever go to the effort of actually changing how people work. We talk about changing. We send out emails exhorting people to change. We encourage change. But we never install and control real process change. So, we never really get the results we know are possible. This is going to be heavy-lifting for you and your team, no doubt about it. You can't leave your conference room until you have lined out process steps for your experiment that will change the way people work.

If you determine that there is no ready, available, or reliable measurement in place that can unequivocally attest to the success of your change, then go back to the drawing board. Revisit the prioritization matrix again and pick another project. If you cannot measure the impact of your experiment's change, you cannot build a case for broader implementation and adoption in the business. And why would you want to do that anyway? Radical impact is always measurable. If you can't get a number on it, it is not a solvable business problem.

YOU SIMPLY MUST HAVE AN EXPERIMENT THAT CAN BE MEASURED. OTHERWISE, YOU ARE WASTING YOUR TIME.

You and your team should have your experiment plan written and pitch-"ready." You don't need to build a doctoral dissertation, but you do need a coherent document that defines the experiment you want to execute. You need a minimum viable process or procedure, just enough to communicate to others what is about to happen. After you write the proposal, you have to do something a little scary. If you are running an experiment beyond your current scope of authority, then you must gain authorization to run the experiment.

SPONSOR PITCH

Armed with a clear strategic statement and a concise and minimal execution plan for a small prototype experiment, it is time to pitch your authorizing sponsor. More often than not, you will receive a series of questions you had not thought of in your team's conference room questions. These questions from a sponsoring authority are valuable because that vetting allows you to hone your prototype. You might be fortunate enough to have a sponsoring authority who takes this collaborative and vetting approach with you and your team. More than likely, however, your sponsoring authority will be mired in the status quo, a surrogate of the dragon, who kills off any attempt at real radical impact.

If you face such an authority, your pitch to prototype a solution will be met by the sponsoring authority with two experiment-killing tactics. First, he or she will request more detailed analysis and modeling. Your attempts to actually change how work is done will be mired in endless analysis loops. This is the famous "analysis paralysis" that kills off progress in business. The reality is many great prototypes die right here. If you run into this attack, you would be best served to go back to your list and find a project with a more forward-thinking sponsoring authority. Second, such a dragon-keeping authority will attempt to build a broad consensus too early in the process. Even if your experiment is small with a relatively low impact on the broader business (or no impact) if the prototype does not work perfectly (which it won't), many sponsoring authorities will not approve a prototype without getting consensus authority from either their cross-functional peers or their own bosses. Consensus-building at this point is a waste of time. Everyone's predisposed affection with the status quo will kill off your prototype. Sponsoring authorities use this technique so that someone else, besides themselves, says no. Again, if you run into this tactic, it is best to go back to the list and find a project that will go around this personnel road block.

Remember, you are waking up the dragon of the status quo as soon as you leave the conference room with an execution plan. It will use everything it's got, at this point, to stop you. The reality of radical impact hunting is you will have to be resourceful and resilient. This is how radical impact happens, one attempt, one wire at a time.

You might have wonderful sponsoring authorities who will green light your prototype with minimal interference. These sponsoring authorities will vet your experiment and be there for support. With their authorization, it is time to take your strategy and execution plan and launch your prototype into the live business. In prototyping you shift from strategy to obsessive execution. Now, you will have really stirred up the status quo and that's when all hell will break loose.

SEVEN: ADJUSTING

THE EDISON BULB

On the corner of my desk I keep a replica of Thomas Edison's light bulb. It is my desk lamp. Thomas Edison was a true business creative. He held a wad of patents, invented prolifically, and started companies like General Electric. He did not subscribe to the myths of business education like I addressed in part one of this book. He had about three months of formal education in his entire life, but he was an autodidact, and he was brilliant.

Edison iterated tirelessly as he worked to create a commercially viable and patentable light bulb. He knew that it wasn't enough just to invent a light bulb. Other people were attempting that at the time. He wanted a light bulb that could be shared, sold, and brought to the masses. Out of this effort of endless shortfalls, Edison quipped, "I have not failed, I've just found 10,000 ways that won't work." Edison knew in his gut that each failure brought him closer to his goal. All he had to do was keep experimenting, keep showing up, and keep working hard, and he would eventually achieve his goal of inventing a commercially viable light bulb. In 1880 he patented the world's first commercially viable light bulb, and it changed the world forever.

Here you are. You have your first experiment, your prototype, ready to go. You are wise enough to not take the dragon head on, but you have to start the process, and you are starting it now. Likely, probably, predictably, your first attempts in your small experiment will be full of holes. That's why we are starting small, so that we can fail small. I know that businesses abhor and punish failure. You are not in the safe confines of Edison's lab. You are out there, exposed and vulnerable. This first entry into radical impact creation and its preordained and necessary failure can be unnerving. Your first instinct will be to roll up your sleeping bag, throw on your backpack, apologize to the offended, and retreat to the delusional safety of the farm or the fort. No! Not when you are this close to radical impact. Yes, you are this close. Depending on the complexity of your experiment, you could be within weeks of changing the course of your team, department, business, and your career. You are on the precipice of changing the way you work forever.

I have tried and failed at creating radical impact more times than I can remember. My career was born out of a balance sheet of more successes than failures, and nothing more. I tell clients and groups that I have failed at everything that they will ever try. I am an enlightened guru, but I keep trying, keep showing up, and keep working hard, and push through the failures. As I consider Edison's light bulb and the paradoxical relationship it illuminates of failure and ground-breaking achievement, I am drawn to another thread of Edison's thinking when he said, "Many of life's failures are people who did not realize how close they were to success when they gave up."

If, when you launch your prototype, it goes horribly wrong, then celebrate the fact that you are closer to the dragon's death. If you are not fired for the mess or your pay is not cut you are closer. If you adjust the prototype, debug it, mess it up, and adjust it again, you are closer. In the rest of this chapter I will show you some areas that will typically need adjusting with this guarantee. If you keep adjusting your prototype, don't let off until it is ready for "prime time." Give it every ounce of yourself. If you do so, you will solve radical impact. That's when the light bulbs will really go on!

WHY ALL RADICAL IMPACT SOLUTIONS ARE CUSTOM JOBS

You will recall from the first part of the book that I addressed the myth of the "new" and the world of the "best practice." I introduced the idea that radical impact solutions for your business can't be found in the best practices of other businesses or in search engine results.

> All **RADICAL IMPACT** solutions are custom jobs that rely on collaboration and experimentation rather than connectivity and search results.

Why can't we piggy back on other people's work in their companies? There are two types of problems in most businesses: 1) the problems that can be found in all businesses and 2) the problems unique to a specific business. When you recognize this fact, you will find that the solutions that separate a business from its peers are the solutions that address problems unique to that specific business. When we solve problems that can be found in all businesses of the same species, we find level and stable performance. We join the club of our industry or segment. We have paid the table stakes that make us a real player, but we are still "me, too." The real difference between a top-performing business and a "me, too" business is that a top-performing business has solved the problems that make it unique in the world and to its customers. Its radical impact solutions are all custom jobs.

The challenges you are facing with your prototype solution fall into one of these two buckets: 1) problems everyone has and 2) problems unique to your company. Let's walk through a few of these problems so that you can hone your prototype and get it ready for the big show.

PROBLEMS WITH PROCESSES

You have launched your prototype process and/or procedure to focus your marketing effort for selling more light bulbs. In your prototype, you are attempting to send out targeted email blasts to customers who have bought light bulbs less frequently than other customers of the same type. You are limiting your experiment to your Cleveland facility. Your working theory is that if you email blast these infrequent customers, you should see an increase in light bulb sales in Cleveland. You have decided to run this experiment for thirty days, simple enough.

But after the first week of the experiment, light bulb sales have declined. You could apologize, or you can dig in and adjust. Results in the first few days of a new process often can get worse. Let's work on understanding why so that we can adjust the prototype to get the results we want.

Here are some common failure points for prototypes for you to weigh.

BAD DATA

Did you have the right target email list to begin with? Customer Relationship Management (CRM) software can be riddled with errors. Did you scrub your list of email blast recipients personally, or did you assume the information personnel got it right?

A prototype is no time to delegate. If ever there is a time to micro-manage, it is during prototype. Many a prototype has blown up on the launch pad because the data used in the prototype was not good. The good news is you can clean it up and re-launch. Get scrubbing.

BAD MEASUREMENT

In an attempt to measure improved light bulb sales in Cleveland, you might discover that the way you have been measuring light bulb sales in Cleveland all these years has been wrong all along. This is a measurement and a data issue. The status quo wants us to believe that every measurement is reliable, repeatable, and indisputable. The fact of the matter is that many legacy measurements in your businesses are full of problems. Just because everyone has used the same dial to tell them the same thing for the last ten years doesn't mean the dial is correct.

For instance, you might find in this prototype that you have not classified your light bulbs correctly, so to speak. You could be calling bulbs that are fluorescent type bulbs "incandescent bulbs" or vice-versa. You could discover that you are calling the same light bulb different things, so that you are diluting the sales dollars in both names. A client I was working with had a number one selling part called "miscellaneous." How do you create sales improvement in "miscellaneous?"

The trap here is that you shut down the prototype to fix data and measurement. Instead, scrub the data enough to get your experiment working, but you don't need to fix the whole data and measurement system of your business. Make a list of "discovery" items that will identify the whole laundry list of data issues you discover in your scrub. Present them when you report or evaluate your prototype's results, but fix what you need to get the prototype back on track.

LATENCY

You may not have a problem with your prototype at all. It may just be a matter of waiting. Often a result is latent to the action we take. People get busy; maybe the customers you sent the email blast to hadn't read it yet. Maybe they have it in their "to do" list for next week. If you overreact to a latency issue, you will pull the rug out from under the experiment. Have you implemented a marketing initiative in the past that has taken some time to get rolling? Lean on that knowledge and wait.

Though a prototype is a relatively short business experiment, it could take a few days for the results of the effort to create a measurable impact.

CONFOUNDS

A confound occurs in an experiment when a result can't be attributed to what you were trying to achieve. In this specific prototype, we are trying to prove that sending out an email blast to dormant light bulb customers will increase light bulb sales in Cleveland. Yet, we observe that one week after we have launched our experiment, light bulb sales have actually decreased. We have cleaned up our data and measurements and are still showing a real light bulb decrease. We know we need to be patient because of the latency effect, but we don't want to just sit around hoping that the orders for light bulbs will start rolling in. As you sit around the conference room commiserating, it hits you. Cleveland had a big snow storm in the first week of the experiment. Many schools and offices were shut down for the better part of the week. Unless your intended email blast recipients were working remotely, they did not get a chance to receive your email blast. Now that your recipients are back to work, they will have a chance to respond.

The snowstorm is an experimental "confound," and it is driving a false negative reading in your results. If you don't identify confounds you will make a classic error. You will adjust your prototype to respond to the "confound." If you make this error you will, at the end, have solved for a very specific, but wrong, solution. In this example, if you respond to the confound you will solve for "how to sell more light bulbs during a snowstorm."

Don't solve for confounds. Instead, identify them and reset. One way to identify the effect of the confound in this specific experiment is to look at light bulb sales in total. If the snowstorm is a confound, it should have impacted all of your light bulb sales. Your entire sales volume should be down, not just that for your slower customers. Confounds can work in the positive as well and thereby trick us into thinking our experiment is a success when really it has been confounded in the positive direction. Let's say that despite the snowstorm, light bulb sales in dormant customers shot up in Cleveland one week after your email blasts.

Time to celebrate and expand the experiment? Not so fast. You must study your success. Remember, radical impact, by definition, is a sustainable result. That means the result must continue forever. If your email blast is really responsible for the uptick in sales, then great, you and your team have a created sustainable fix by installing more focused marketing effort. But, what if, unbeknownst to you and your team, the marketing team had launched a sale on light bulbs the week you launched your email blast experiment. Was the uptick in sales caused by your email blast or a reduced sale price? There is no way to know. The experiment has been confounded.

If you misread this uptick, you are making another classic mistake. You are confusing correlation with causality. The uptick in light bulb sales is happening at the same time as your email blast. Your email blast and sales of light bulbs are happening in the same time and place. They are correlated, but your uptick in light bulb sales is not directly caused by the email blast. You can't establish causality because the experiment was confounded by the sale price marketing put out on light bulbs. If you confuse correlation with causality, you will claim success in the experiment and will be embarrassed when it is attempted in another more expanded version and fails.

In your experiment, it is critical that you address the impacts of confounds and clearly understand the difference between correlation and causality. It does you no good to claim success for an experiment that is not repeatable or sustainable. You haven't killed the dragon of the status quo if you have not established sustainability.

VARIATION

Think about the cruise control on your car. Have you ever noticed that when you use cruise control while you drive that you get better gas mileage then when you don't use cruise control? Why is that? When you are driving with your foot on the gas paddle, even on the highway on a long drive, you are making significant adjustments on the accelerator. Every time you make a significant adjustment to speed up, you burn more fuel. If you let off the accelerator too much and have to compensate to get back up to speed, then again, more fuel burn. Cruise control is digitally driven, so adjustments to speeding up and slowing down are more precise and smaller. By making smaller adjustments that are more precise, the cruise control system burns less fuel in the act of speeding up and slowing down. Cruise control removes variability from fuel burn on your drive, giving you better and more predictable gas mileage.

Variation is a natural occurrence. We will never eliminate it. Our very evolution as a species depends on the variation that occurs in our genetic code. But we want to control and mitigate the effects of variation in our business experiment as much as we reasonably can. When we control variation we control outcome.

This tenet of controlling variation to control outcome is the fundamental tenet of the quality control system known as Six Sigma. Six Sigma, invented by Motorola and Americanized by General Electric, is a methodology obsessed with identifying and eliminating variation so that a process delivers near-perfect output every single time it is utilized. Six Sigma is a great tool to use to identify and solve for process variation. However, you do not need to be an expert in Six Sigma to solve for variation in your experiment right now. You just need to understand a little about variation's impact on your outcome and how to mitigate or control its effects.

Let's say you have sent an email blast to all dormant light bulb customers under the working theory that the email blast will get those customers' attention and they will buy more light bulbs. To solve for variation, you must first have a measurable goal in mind that is more specific than just the sales volume increase you are hoping for. Sales volume can raise several issues related to variation. For example, your dormant customer may respond to your email blast by calling customer service to place a light bulb order. Maybe customer service is busy that day and your dormant responder has to stay on hold too long. He hangs up the phone and does not place an order. Did your email blast work or was your marketing experiment a failure? If you measure that email blast only in terms of the sales volume it created then "no" it did not. To solve the experiment of the email blast as a revenue driving tool, for example, you must identify and control all of the variables that could give you a false negative. You need to unequivocally prove that email blasts to dormant customers drive sales.

You don't make radical impact by describing variation. Your experiment drives radical impact when it drives real double-digit revenue increases and not until then. Yet if you do not isolate and solve for the variation that detracts from your revenue experiment, it will never have the radical impact you are shooting for. Think of all the other things that can cause a customer respondent not to order light bulbs from you, even though they have responded to your email blast:

- You might not have enough of the light bulbs they want to order available.
- Your pricing may not be competitive.
- They might have a delivery requirement you can't execute.
- They might have special packaging requirements.
- The brand of light bulb you carry may not be the brand they require.

Some of these variables will have more impact on your results than others. Some of these variables will have little impact at all. Knowing which ones have impact and which ones don't deserve attention is as much an art as a science. When you have performed a thousand radical IMPACT cycles, you'll get a feel for it. The key point is this: Solving for the variations that matter is solving your experiment. This is one of the ways radical impact happens, by solving for variation within your experiment. That's why we don't need to spend an inordinate amount of time picking the experiment we are going to work on. Because once we are on the scent of radical impact, we will get to it one way are the other. The important thing is not the experiment we pick but the result we generate. In this experiment, you set out to prove that email blasts to dormant customers improve light bulb sales, and you will prove that. As you solve your experiment and solve for variation in it, you also will develop solutions to call-hold time, inventory positioning, pricing, delivery options, packaging, and branding. As you solve these variables you will see that your email blast is just the starting point to the double-digit revenue increase you have just created.

WASTE

In 1996, when James Womack and Daniel Jones launched their landmark book *Lean Thinking* into the American business world, they opened the book with a discussion on the impact "waste" has on business performance. The business improvement methodology known as "Lean" has been around long enough and has had enough success stories that it should be integral in our business problem-solving lexicon. Yet, the methodology and terminology that accompanies it still rests in the margins of most middle managers' problem-solving set.

One of the things I observe when I am in a middle manager's work area are the books that they keep handy. I nearly always see a copy of Womack and Jones' groundbreaking book within reach. Yet, when I ask them how they solve for *muda* in their department or business, they look at me as if I am speaking, well, Japanese. I usually have to fight off the urge to tell these managers and executives that *muda* is the Japanese word for "waste." Waste is what is driving much of their underperformance, and *muda* is the first word in the Womack and Jones book on their shelf.

If your experiment is struggling to provide the results you intended, you must solve not only for variation but also for waste. These two performance killers, variation and waste, are the footholds of the status quo. Eliminate variation and waste, and the status quo becomes wobbly, vulnerable, and beatable.

Six Sigma (the science of eliminating variation) and Lean (the process of eliminating waste) are tools, not silver bullets. They are extremely effective at eliminating the footholds of the status quo on business performance. Yes, they can be highly technical. Yes, they can be a little too "jargon"-driven (they both have their own terminology and language). Yes, they are techniques that are challenging to master. But every artist and every scientist has had to master difficult techniques in order to get their life's work done. The biggest waste I see in middle management today is that even though every aspiring business creative is capable of mastering techniques such as Six Sigma and Lean, these business creatives do not receive or take the opportunity to master the techniques because, well, they are difficult to master.

Mozart isn't Mozart if he doesn't master the technique of music theory. F. Scott Fitzgerald is not F. Scott Fitzgerald if he doesn't master the technique of compelling narrative. Claude Monet is not Claude Monet if he doesn't master the technique of light-influenced landscapes. If you don't master these techniques, you are wasting too much career time trying to solve problems whereas appropriate application of technique would easily help you break through to the solution.

I worked with a team that had spent months struggling on a problem. While trying to achieve higher warehouse inventory accuracy, they were not willing to spend the money for a barcoding system. No matter what they tried, they could not improve their accuracy. I flew down to see them. We walked to their warehouse. I took out a sheet of paper and drew out for them what they should do. It took me five minutes, and it worked immediately. Was I a genius? No. My prescriptive solution worked because I knew the technique to apply. In this case it was a "5S" solution right out of the Lean textbooks.

If your experiment is under-performing and if you have solved for variation, then the next place to look is at the areas that waste *(muda)* can ruin a process. Look for areas in which the experiment is constantly having to be reworked. In our light bulb sales experiment, this could be happening in our email blast contact list. If we are constantly having to scrub and rescrub the contact list so that our email blast gets to the right customer, then that is rework. Focus on how to get that list right the first time. Is there a checklist we could create that would scrub the contact list before we started email blasting? Rework takes six times longer than getting work done right the first time. In an experiment, we need to go fast. We need to get results on the board so that we can broaden the experiment. We can't do that if we are constantly being thrown into rework loops.

Look for areas of waste in your experiment that have to do with inventories. In this experiment, do you have too much of the light bulbs no one is asking for and too little of the light bulbs everyone wants? If so, you are creating inventory waste. Inventory doesn't have to be hard goods. You could have too many customer service representatives in a call center, draining resources away from other areas that would benefit from the investment. You could have empty office or warehouse space that you are paying for, draining capital away from game-changing investments. Anywhere you have too much of something that is not creating a return on its investment, you have inventory waste.

Look for areas in your experiment in which you have approval or double-checking loops. This is an endemic area of waste across most underperforming businesses. I once worked with a CEO of a mid-sized company who had a policy that he must approve every purchase order that the company placed to suppliers. An activity that took him several hours a week. It held up the entire organization while he mulled over these purchases. "Do you ever disapprove any of these purchase orders?" I asked. "No," he said. He just wanted his employees to know–or think–he was paying attention. We freed up hours of his and his staff's time by eliminating this approval loop and replacing it with an exception-based report.

In the email blast to sell light bulbs experiment, are you entering information twice or having to get sign-offs? These are target-rich environments to eliminate waste and get on with the business of producing real results.

Approval loops, double-checking, and double-entry create another area of waste in processes that limit performance–the waste of waiting. The theory of constraints says that no process can go faster than its slowest step. Waiting creates bottlenecks in processes and those bottlenecks exponentially compound the wasted time throughout the remainder of the process. Eliminate waiting time from processes, and you will fly toward your improved results.

I do not intend here to oversimplify Lean and Six Sigma. However, if you want to master radical impact hunting, then you must master these two critical business improvement techniques. For the purposes of our discussion and for progressing in our experiment, it is sufficient to have an understanding that underperformance in our experiment can be rooted out and solved by eliminating variation and waste. Once we have solved for variation and waste in the experiment itself, we can solve one of the big variables that cause more experiments to fail than any other variable.

ADOPTION

As you bob and weave through the adjustments you need to make in your experiment to "prove out" its validity in creating radical impact, you must never keep far from your mind that you have an active, clever, and destructive enemy in the status quo. That dragon will let you meander through the simple process fixes that we have just discussed. You can sneak up on it by working through your bad data, bad measurement, latency, and confound issues. But as soon as you hit it in the knees by eliminating the real issues, variation, and waste, you have the dragon's attention and concern. He knows you are now a serious threat, and he will throw the kitchen sink at you. He will look at you and your little team of prototype hounds, and he will grow angry with your progress. After all, the dragon knows that very few radical impact hunts ever get this far. The status quo hates to work, so it will let everyone else in your business do the work for it. You and your team may have the heart for the fight, but the rest of the business doesn't. The dragon of the status quo has them by the throat, and he won't give them up easily.

The first line of attack for the status quo is to fight off adoption of your prototype process. It knows that if you don't get enough process cycles through your prototype, then you can't prove out that your new process works. If you can't prove that the prototype process works, then you can't codify it and transition it into the broader business. Codifying and transitioning are the last two phases of the radical IMPACT cycle. These two final steps seal the dragon in its cave forever and leave it there to rot. The dragon knows this. So it will fight tooth, nail, and fire to keep you and your team from exiting the "adjust" phase of your solution.

You simply must get people to comply with your new prototype process. In the prototype example we have been working through, you must get the marketing team to send out email blasts to dormant customers, which means some analyst is going to have to give them a list of dormant light bulb customers. As you solve for variation and waste, you must get the inventory personnel to stock the right light bulbs so that you can sell the light bulbs dormant customers want. You must get the customer service team to answer the phone faster. The list of tasks and steps that other people must execute for your simple prototype to "prove out" can get unwieldy. And not one of those team members will want to help you. They are too busy working on their own departmental chicken farms and forts.

Unfortunately, the tomes of treatment on the subject matter of change management won't help you much here. Change management, by the book, takes too long. You don't have time to make a case to each and every person of "what's in it for them" if they help you. Sometimes, "nothing is in it" for them in the short term. You are in prototype, and the longer it takes, the less chance it is has of succeeding.

In Marine Corps boot camp, I was required to rappel off of a one-hundred-foot tower. I didn't want to. This is where the drill instructor came in. The Marine Corps drill instructor is a genius at change management. He knows that the only way to get a guy like me to jump backwards off of a one-hundred-foot tower is to make it more uncomfortable to stay on top of the tower than to jump off it. The genius of his change management technique is in what the drill instructor does not try to accomplish. He has nothing to do with and no desire to cure my fear of heights. That's not his job. His change management job is to get me from "on the tower" to "off the tower," period. He accomplishes that with great proficiency.

Is his technique elegant? No. Will I send him a Christmas card? No. Did he get me to overcome the status quo? Yes.

COMPETENCY

It is six o'clock on a Thursday afternoon, and I am working with a purchasing manager on tactics to improve first-pass order fill rates in his business. The business he is in relies on the right part being in the right place at the right time. If those conditions don't consistently exist, then his business loses customers to the competition. I have worked with him for a couple of months, and we are both getting frustrated. The key performance indicators we are using to measure the effectiveness of his tactics are not budging. I am scratching my head. Every tactic I have given him has worked every time I have used them anywhere I have ever worked ever. Why aren't they working here? What am I missing? I decide to have him walk me through his decisions and tactics in a couple of "case" scenarios and, there, the problem manifested itself. He was doing the tactics wrong, again. There was nothing wrong with the tactics or my teaching of the tactics. This purchasing manager simply could not work at the level of competency that the tactics required. It happens. Sometimes, even if people will adopt your prototype, they will not be competent enough to make it work. It sounds harsh, but sometimes people just can't be trained, taught, or tricked into doing a job right.

After I had reviewed my training techniques with this purchasing manager, I concluded he could not master the necessary tactics. His inability didn't make him a bad person or someone to be eliminated from the company. It just meant that we had bumped up against his cognitive bandwidth. I have the same issue with calculus. As much as I want to learn it, and as many times as I have tried, I just can't. It is beyond my cognitive capability. When we run up against personal limits in the prototype phase of the radical

IMPACT cycle, we need to quickly shed our optimism, and find competent people. You can kill a project in constant retraining of staff.

The status quo will challenge you. It will create doubt by suggesting that if you can't get a team up to speed on your tiny insignificant prototype, how could you ever expect to get people up to speed in the broader business? You don't. In prototype, you don't know who is capable of what until you let them try out the work in the prototype you have created. It may be that your prototype is overcomplicated and hard to execute, or you may have staff members who, in the status quo world of your business would be assigned to a "fix" like the one you are testing, but lack the capability to actually execute it. This is an opportunity to bring other talented team members to the forefront. Let them take a shot at it, regardless of what the organizational chart says their job is. The status quo wants you to stay within the artificial boundaries of people's current capabilities and within the arbitrary deployment of resources your organizational chart dictates. Don't fall into that trap. It will kill your prototype. Get people working in your experiment that can actually demonstrate the outcome of the experiment.

So what happened to the fill rate experiment with the less-than-capable purchasing manager? In the meetings we held on the topic, a young lady who had been hired as administrative support sat in. She was relatively quiet and reserved, but she never missed a meeting and took voracious notes. Sensing the opportunity when we had reached a performance road block she spoke up. "Would it be possible for me to take a try at these tactics?" Her logic was that by letting her try she would free up the purchasing manager to focus on the day-to-day work. He was ecstatic and abdicated his role in the experiment immediately. I have never seen someone exit a meeting room and race back to the arms of the status quo more quickly than that purchasing manager did that day.

But, then something amazing happened. Not only did this quiet administrative support person understand the tactics; she also executed them with a professional deftness that demonstrated that she was paying attention and wanted the experiment to work. Within ninety days of her involvement, the prototype had been expanded into the broader business and the fill rate challenge of that company had been solved. She was the one who did it. She was promoted twice in two years and her income has nearly doubled, because she spoke up, engaged, and developed competency.

That is radical impact. That is I AM.

What happened to the purchasing manager? He was removed from his position and reassigned.

During the adjusting phase of the radical IMPACT cycle, an opportunity is created for people. This opportunity is created for any staff member anywhere in the organization to join the hunt and to help win the war against the status quo. There are people in your business right now who have the innate competencies you need to get your prototype through the adjusting phase. Don't turn your prototype into an endless training loop by hanging on to people who can't get you there. The "adjust" phase of the radical IMPACT cycle is no place for staff development of the incapable. Work to find people you need, recruit them, put them to work, and watch your prototype move forward.

POLITICS

Prototypes fail when they fail to connect effort with results. That failure is baked into this scope-creeping invitation. After all, one of the reasons you are creating radical impact is to help launch you to new levels of achievement in your career. If you bite off and accommodate the boss's scope creep, then your prototype will fail. That new international division will never materialize, and you will be put back in your place, captive to the status quo.

Avoid the attention of the bosses at all costs during the adjusting phase of your prototype. Your adjustments depend on sustained and focused effort, not flattery. Then, after you have solved for your prototype, you will be ready to roll it out in all its radical impact-creating glory. Keep your prototype tight on scope, and keep it progressing toward your intended result. Solve one true thing and the rest of the good stuff will come along. The politics and power structure of your business will work against you the closer you get to achieving your results. The status quo will use coercion, brute force, and flattery to get you out of the hunt. Don't bend.

EXITING THE ADJUSTING PHASE

At this point in the adjust phase, we have overcome every major obstacle the status quo has thrown at our prototype. We can now say unequivocally that email blasting dormant customers has a significant and sustainable impact on light bulb sales in Cleveland. Getting to this point, a tested and validated prototype will be the hardest thing you will ever do in business. They get easier as you go along, but it is always hard. As you conclude the adjusting phase, you and your team are solving one of the toughest middle management challenges there is in nature: creating radical impact where none previously existed.

This is no small thing, but let's get perspective on where you are in the radical IMPACT cycle. You are so much better at middle management than you were just a few short weeks ago. Though it may still feel awkward, and you may be a little skinned up from the battle of it, you have become more adept. For you to sink the blade into the throat of this dragon you must take two more steps through the radical IMPACT cycle. Stop here, and the dragon will swat your effort away as little more than an irritant. You will have flirted with radical impact but will not have sealed the deal. Keep going, and you win.

EIGHT: CODIFYING

You have duplicated the trial and effort that traditional art-ists and scientists experience to bring an idea to life. Bruised and battered as you may feel right now, your quest is still unrealized. Your successful prototype is the equivalent of a writer's rough draft, a painter's sketchbook, or a musician's studio tapes. You are close but not yet there. The dragon of the status quo is teetering but rallying for one final strike at the heart of your effort. Now, it is time to codify your proto-type. Codifying makes your prototype publisher-, gallery-, and iTunes-ready. The world is waiting.

ISO DOCUMENTATION IS NOT CODIFYING THE BUSINESS

I was working with a mid-size hardware distributor in the Northeast. They bought and sold hundreds of millions of dollars' worth of nuts and bolts every year and made good money doing it. The problem was that they were losing customers at an alarming rate. All of the components for customer loyalty existed in their business with the exception of one thing. They could not ship customer orders on time. The only thing consistent about this company's delivery dates was that they were consistently late.

I showed up to their regional headquarters on a crisp New England fall day. I had arrived the day before this office's International Organization for Standards or ISO audit, and they could not locate all of the ISO manuals. ISO requires that all of a business's processes be documented and adhered to so that a business can control the output of those processes. It sounds great in theory, but in reality the ISO system of documentation control had calcified into a closed loop system of company specialists, outside consultants, and certifying bodies. Most of how a business operates has very little to do with their ISO documentation on a day-in, day-out basis. In this environment, ISO is just a "check box" of compliance to an industry standard. That's when the manuals get lost.

It turns out that this hardware company had attained ISO certification in order to meet the requirements necessary to sell to exactly one of their customers. None of their other customers required the certification. They did find their manuals and they did cram enough to pass their audit, but it was not until we dug into the nuts and bolts of their processes and iterated through the radical IMPACT cycle that we solved their on-time delivery challenges. You cannot rely on ISO documentation as codification of your radical impact fixes. You are changing your business on the fly. ISO documentation is outdated the second you get results in your prototype. You must codify your solution to get it out of your head, out of your team, and into the broader business. And you must codify quickly, before the dragon knows what hit it.

CODIFYING TOOL #1: THE POWER OF POLICY

The fastest path to codifying your successful prototype into the broader business is through an authoritative policy statement. Depending on the culture and size of your business this statement could be relatively easy or extremely difficult. You have already installed the controls necessary to insure that your prototype solution works as advertised. If you can get a clear and directive policy statement to codify your solution into the broader business, you should be able to control compliance and demonstrate radical impact. For example, the boss is so impressed that emailing dormant Cleveland customers has impacted light bulb sales that she decides to make this a national policy. She may put out a statement to the business that says something such as, "All locations will email blast all dormant light bulb customers on a quarterly basis. Our radical impact team will train you on the details of how this works." Codification by policy can be that simple. Empowered by a simple policy statement, you and your team would shift out of prototype mode and into training and adoption mode.

Consider this example. I was working with a client who had as part of their sales model a sourcing component. The pitch to their customer base went something such as, "If we don't carry it, we will go out and find it. We are your one stop shop." Nearly half of the client's revenue came from sourcing products they did not normally carry for their customer base. One source of tension: hurried customers often ordered the wrong thing. The customer then requested of the client a product return (due to customer error). The customer-sensitive client almost always accepted returns on these sourced products. You can imagine the problem this procedure created. The client's significant investment in sourcing staff increased with the high volume of returns. In addition, much of the sourced product could not be returned to the source. So, the client's warehouses were bursting with "one-off" inventory. This hyper-responsiveness to customers was drying up the client's cash flow and bottom line profitability.

The solution? First, the client formed a team that ran an experiment. The experiment focused on a slice of the customer base to test the impact of charging a restock fee for sourced material that was returned. This experiment demonstrated that the client could charge customers a restock fee for sourced material without impacting that customer's future business with the client. Although the client's salesforce resisted this experiment, the team prevailed and proved the prototype's success. The company president met with the team, examined the results, and then issued a policy statement: "All returns from customers for sourced material will contain a twenty percent restock fee. Any deviation from this policy must be approved by me."

In that simple policy statement, the client changed its cash flow and bottom line profitability math. They earned enough money on restock fees to dispose of returned material and paid for a significant amount of the cost of the sourcing team. When brought to scale, this simple codifying act of a policy statement transitioned a prototype into the broader business and delivered real and sustainable radical impact to the client.

Obviously, the smaller the business the easier it is to move from a proven prototype to a policy statement from the boss. However, this codifying tactic is too quickly dismissed in larger businesses, and they miss out on the rapid scaling of radical impact solutions. Why do larger businesses avoid the policy directive statement as a means to rapid codification of a radical impact solution? They tend to avoid this tactic because they have an over-reliance on the false comfort that consensus building brings. In larger companies that rely on consensus-building as a change agent, the proven prototype that you and your team have worked so hard to solidify will have to be vetted and re-vetted by various stakeholder groups. In other words, the experiment will have to be replicated, duplicated, and justified. Consensus-building at this stage is nothing more than the status quo dragon masked as inclusion. Suffice it to say, when you present your proven prototype and the boss says, "Let's get consensus on this," you can bet on a long slog and also that a bold policy statement will probably never happen.

But, you still must codify your prototype. Otherwise, it remains an interesting experiment. If you can't get a policy statement done, then it is time to move toward several other process solution tools.

CODIFYING TOOL #2: SOFTWARE PROCESSES

I am going to make a twenty-first century assumption that your business is operating on some kind of software platform. I am assuming that your customer relationships, order fulfillment, product development, and financial processes are software-based. If that is the case, then you can codify your proven prototype through software rules and steps. For example, in our dormant customer experiment for light bulbs, you could set up your customer relationship software to email blast dormant customers without any human intervention at all. This is simply a matter of programming in rules and parameters. By codifying your prototype into software you achieve flawless accuracy, consistency, and efficiency in its execution. You achieve accuracy because most software usually minimizes (though rarely if ever eliminates) errors. You achieve consistency because software won't forget to do something. You also achieve efficiency because once the setup is done, there is no human effort required to assure compliance. In the techniques of both Six Sigma for variation and Lean for waste elimination, this act of codifying a prototype into a software process improves chances of "fool-proofing" the process. It radically reduces human error as a reason for missing the mark on radical impact.

In the example of the client who created a policy for restock fees, a software process was developed to "fool-proof" execution of the policy. In this client example, when a customer service person entered a customer return for sourced material into the business system, the system would not allow the customer service person to issue the return authorization to the customer without the restock fee being entered as a charge on the return. That way, no return authorization was ever issued to a customer for sourced material that did not comply with policy.

For most of you, your early attempts at radical impact are going to be fairly easy to codify into software rules. Even if programming costs a chunk of time and money, your prototype is designed to create radical impact in revenue, profitability, cash, service, or product innovation. Rally support and get the programmers to work.

CODIFYING TOOL #3: PROCESS DOCS

As the previous two codify tools demonstrate, codification can be as simple as a policy statement or as complicated as software rules. The middle ground of difficulty and expense is the process document. Again, most of your early attempts at completing the radical IMPACT cycle will be in process re-engineering or improvement. You will tend to focus on a pain factor that if eliminated would create radical impact, and in that arena you will be attacking how work is done at your level in the business, often for levels downstream at your business, and rarely (for the extremely daring) for levels above you in the business. Whenever you are attacking "how" work is done, you are usually in the process world.

You can attack processes in any of the five key areas of radical impact. You can improve the process of growing revenue. Our example of emailing dormant customers to improve light bulb sales is an example of this kind of process. You can improve the process of optimizing profitability in any number of process attacks that eliminate variation and waste. You can improve the process of creating cash through the "how" of asset management and financial processes. You can improve the processes that create differentiation. And you can improve the processes that are involved in bringing product innovation to the market. But if you don't codify your process fixes, you relegate your project to "tribal knowledge." That's not scalable or sustainable, and that's not radical impact.

Process documentation is relatively straight forward. There are software tools to pretty it up and track changes that are made in the future, but a process document need not be its own science project. Depending on the type of business you are in, you may need to involve your quality management system personnel in documenting your prototype. Many businesses prioritize high control of documenting processes and modifying documents. This control is not without warrant as failure to properly control documentation can lead to business confusion or loss of industry certifications such as ISO. The benefits of your radical impact solution far outweigh the difficulties of navigating internal bureaucracy. Find out the rules, jump through the hoops, and codify your solution.

Whether you have a formal documentation control system or an informal one, your process document should contain a few basic elements so that your prototype solution will achieve its intended result: Your process document should have a table of contents and a statement of purpose. Explain in detail why anyone should pay attention to this new way of working.

- Write processes in a way that anyone who has been in the business at least ninety days would be able to execute the process without getting anyone else involved. Your process documentation needs to be that simple and that clear.

- Avoid complicated language. Strip words down to their simplest terms. Use readability score software tools and write you process to read at eighth- to tenth-grade level.

- Explain and define every technical or business specific term.

- D.A.A. (Define All Acronyms)

- If your process requires interaction with software to execute, then painstakingly show through screen shots and steps how to navigate that software without getting lost. This is harder than it looks. We fly through the applications we are familiar with. When you have to break it down into each navigational step, it can get clunky quickly.

I am a huge fan of the process document. I have written dozens of them, from back of the envelope work instructions to one hundred-page departmental directives. Process documents are an extremely effective way to get your prototype codified and get the rest of the business on your radical impact page. The hoops you may have to jump through in order to get your document installed in your quality management system are well worth the effort if your document leads to radical results.

CODIFYING TOOL #4: CHECKLISTS

A checklist is an effective tool for a task-overloaded business. Checklists can be produced and launched quickly, and they are easy to edit on the fly. Editing on the fly will be important in the final phase–"transitioning"–of the radical IMPACT cycle.

Can checklists save lives? Ask Atul Gawande, author of the book *The Checklist Manifesto*. Gawande worked with hospitals all over the world to reduce the amount of infections that patients suffer with after surgery while in the hospital. This is a big problem, and many people die from post-surgical infections. He accomplished the radical impact result of reducing post-operative infection rates and saved lives by developing and installing checklists in surgical procedures.

In my own experience in the world of Marine Corps aviation and as a civilian consumer of air travel, I have witnessed highly trained pilots diligently and methodically executing the same preflight checklists every time they get in the cockpit of an aircraft. There is simply too much at stake for a pilot to rely on memory. You, your peers, and the rest of your business are continually fighting task overload. When you are task-overloaded, you drop details. When you drop details in surgery, people get infections and die. When you drop details in pre-flight of an aircraft, planes tend to end up in places we'd rather they not. And when you drop details in a business process, you detract from business results or lose customers.

Imagine working in a sales company whose lifeblood could be defined by one critical measurement, quote conversion rate. Quote conversion rate is a measurement that compares the amount of quoting a business generates to the amount of orders it wins in a given time period. So if a business executed a hundred quotes in a month and won seventy orders from those quotes, the business's quote conversion rate would be seventy percent (70 orders divided by

100 quotes.). In such a case, improving quote conversion rates could create radical impact.

That's exactly what happened in an industrial sales company in the Southeast. This company's status quo quotes process was typical to many mid-market companies. Every sales person had a highly individualized approach to quoting customers and consequently their quote conversion rates varied widely among individual sales people and varied widely in the business as whole. There was simply no way to use quote conversion rate as a predicative metric for revenue. The metric was descriptive at best and discouraging at worst.

One of the big challenges a mid-market company faces is predictability. If a mid-market company can solve for predictability it can attract capital and grow in a healthy way. Most mid-market companies struggle with predictability because they can't get control of the key levers that determine predictability–in this case, quote conversion rate. Think about this for a minute. If a business can control its quote conversion rate, then the way it can predictably grow revenue is to do two things simultaneously: 1) improve its quote conversion rate and 2) increase the number of quotes that come into the business. To control a process like quoting customers means that every sales person can't have his or her own special way to provide customers quotes. The process must be standardized for some baseline controlled predictability.

One critical factor of quote success for this business was speed of quote. Often the first quote in wins the business. We determined the best solution to control and improve quote conversion rates for this business was to develop a quotes checklist that each salesperson would execute prior to quoting customers. After the quote was provided to the customer, the checklist was turned in to an administrator who made sure all quotes had checklists. That's how compliance with the checklist was controlled. This business had struggled with quote conversion rate control for years. The checklist they used, and still use today, was a single sheet of paper with ten checklist elements on it. It was developed by a cross-functional team of people, tested, debugged, and formalized, from start to finish in four weeks. In the first ninety days after installing the quotes checklist, quote conversion rates had both improved by nearly fifty percent and were controlled at a predictable conversion rate that the business could count on. This resulted in millions of dollars of previously wasted revenue opportunities. This business had fought this battle with the status quo and had lost for years. In four weeks, using the radical IMPACT cycle and the checklist it produced, this team of people killed that dragon for good.

If checklists are good enough for surgeons and pilots, they are probably good enough for us in most businesses.

Checklists are cheap, flexible, fast, and effective. They solve the problem of individual task overload and slow us down at just the right point in our decision-making. When codifying your prototype, try turning your solution into a checklist.

Codifying your prototype solution–whether through policy, software tweaks, process documentation, or check-lists–is the calm before the storm. As you work through these various codifying techniques, you may discover gaps in your solution's capability that did not reveal themselves in the "adjust" phase. Though discouraging, this is the time to circle back in to fix it. You cannot afford to have an intrinsically flawed codified prototype roll out into the larger business. That flaw will be exposed in seconds when brought to business scale. Think of this final piece of codifying adjustment as tightening your helmet, re-lacing your boots, cleaning your weapon one more time, before you and your team launches your final assault on the dragon of the status quo. It is worth an extra few days or even a week or two to make sure your prototype is ready to "hit the beach."

Once codified, you are ready for the big time, transitioning your radical impact solution into the entirety of your business. That's where your final blows to the dragon of the status quo will determine both your fate and the fate of your business's radical impact opportunity.

NINE: TRANSITIONING

My guitar teacher introduces me and motions me to take a position behind the microphone at center stage. My stomach wants to escape from my body, my hands begin to sweat, and I can't remember what it is I am supposed to play. As I walk toward the center of stage, I have two simultaneous thoughts. One, I immediately appreciate every performer I have ever seen who "owns" the stage the second they walk on it. It is harder than it looks, just to walk across a stage and feel like you belong there, let alone like you "own" it. The second thought I have is to breathe.

I had practiced a Freddy King guitar piece called "Hide Away" in my home office for several weeks. Among blues guitar players, Freddy King's "Hide Away," is a "price of admissions" piece. You simply aren't a real blues guitarist if you can't play "Hide Away." Once I had it perfected, my guitar teacher had invited me to play it with his band in a

Sunday night session at no less than The Hard Rock Café in Dallas. I accepted the invitation, because every guitar player wants to play in front of people at some point. I really had perfected that piece of music, in my home office, in front of my desk, and no one else.

On stage, with a band, at The Hard Rock Café was not my home office. The dynamic of playing this well-rehearsed piece had dramatically changed. The piece and my preparation had not. Now, my guitar hero persona needed to "scale up" from my home office to The Hard Rock Café. There was no safety net now. If I messed up, a whole room of people would hear it and think, "Another middle-aged guy trying to be young again." That was not going to happen, was it? I told myself an old adage I had heard at some point in my musical training. "If you are going to screw up, screw up loudly." Hesitancy is the death knell of performance. So, I cranked the volume knob up on my Fender Stratocaster, turned to the band and shouted out, "One, Two, One, Two, Three, Four…"

For three-and-a-half glorious minutes, I channeled Freddy King through my guitar and out to the audience. It sounded so much bigger than in it did in my home office. There were micro-adjustments being made in timing and feel between me and the band throughout the entire piece. At first, this live interplay was unnerving, but my preparation had allowed me to adjust very quickly to the band, and we played well together. About half way through the piece I had forgotten about the location, the lights, the nerves, and just enjoyed playing on a stage. Did I play the piece perfectly? Not even close. I made a big goof toward the end of the piece, but unless you really knew the piece, you probably would not have noticed. I noticed, and the band noticed, and we all made the mental footnote that I needed to work more on that section later. As I landed on the last chord and the drummer's cymbal crash let everyone know we were done, the crowd opened up in enthusiastic applause. I smiled, nodded my head, and left the stage. I had played a guitar solo with a band at The Hard Rock Café. That was a completely different ball game than the hours of playing I had done in my home office. The fundamentals of playing did not change. The scale and the dynamics imposed on the fundamentals by that scale are what changed.

I had scaled my preparation to a larger context.

As you transition your prototype from the codify phase into the larger business, you will encounter scaling issues of your own. Your prototype, along with you and your team, will have to take the stage in the larger business. The fundamentals of your prototype will remain unchanged, but the dynamics imposed by scale of your business will have to be dealt with. It will not be comfortable for you, and the status quo dragon, disguised as perfectionism, will try to keep you stuck in codifying. But for you to realize the radical impact you have worked so hard to create you have to transition your prototype into the larger business context.

In this last step of the radical IMPACT cycle, I will discuss two transitions. The first transition, the transition of your prototype into the larger business, is the most obvious of the two transitions that must occur for radical impact to be delivered by you and your team. The second transition is less obvious but no less critical to codifying radical impact as a cultural norm in yours or any business. For organizations to assimilate radical impact hunting as part of its sustained culture, we must rethink organizational design and alignment. Your prototype sets the example for an overall culture of radical impact, but the organization must make its own journey to broaden the reach of your bold experiment.

THE LARGER BUSINESS CONTEXT

That wheezing sound you hear in the shadows of your business is the dragon of the status quo struggling to hang on to life in your enterprise. With each step you have taken through the radical IMPACT cycle you have dealt that dragon deeper and more damaging blows with your sword of strategic execution. As you exit the 'codify" step of the radical IMPACT cycle, you have placed yourself in a position to finish off this status quo dragon and deliver the radical impact your business needs. The final blow, the one that will finish the dragon off, occurs when you install, roll out, and operationalize your codified prototype into the larger, entire, business platform.

In our example, this means that your initiative can no longer be a Cleveland-selling light bulbs thing. It is time you play on the nationwide stage. Transitioning your prototype from the relatively controlled confines of your team and your journey through the radical IMPACT cycle is an intimidating and unnerving process. First of all, you have to shift from problem solver to change seller. If you think it is difficult driving your status quo dragon to death's door, wait until you try to get people to change the way they work when they carpool with dragons and play in a softball league together. For many people, in many jobs, what they crave, what they want is stability. I can't tell you how many candidates I have eliminated in job interviews over the years because they have answered my standard question, "Why do you want to work here?" with an answer such as, "Because I heard you were a really stable company and I really want a stable job." Hiring the person that answers like this is inviting the dragon into your business. They are status quo seekers and defenders. And you have legions of them in your business right now.

Secondly, you and your team have seen what the radical IMPACT cycle can do. You have experienced the exhilaration of solving a real business problem through to an improved, meaningful, and sustainable result. You have begun a mastery process in strategic execution. You have already created radical impact in your prototype, just not to scale yet. You have created a micro-nuclear explosion in a box in a lab. You have seen the power of what you can unleash. And that will make you impatient with the larger population of the business. This is a dangerous attitude and you will have to fight against it. One of the last, gasping, defenses the status quo will throw it you is to "Shoot the messenger." If you and your team do not methodically and patiently work through your roll out, then you run the risk of having the whole thing shut down because people don't like the way you are delivering the message. You can absolutely lose roll out support and momentum on something as silly as "style points" in your delivery. It has happened to me, and it is a crushing last-minute defeat.

I know you and your team can see the radical impact potential of your prototype. You have done the math and seen big numbers at scale. But, other than perhaps a sponsoring executive, no one else in your business has experienced that "ah ha" moment. They haven't journeyed through the battles of the radical IMPACT cycle with you. They don't know anything about what they are fighting or what is at stake. You have to educate and convince them. You cannot handoff this rollout to a change management team or your sponsoring executive. You are the ones who care and have developed a deep connection to your radical impact solution. You will need to tap every ounce of that intimacy with your solution in order to get other people to sign up and adopt it. Do not hand off the rollout. Own it. Lead it. See it through. The genuineness and sincerity you exude will make all the difference in your prototype's broader adoption in the business platform.

In my experience the best way to manage change is to change. For your prototype to reach its radical impact potential in the total business, you must change the way people work. The best way to do that is through a grassroots approach. Your approach to your broader business should align with the following type of rationale:

- We discovered a dragon in our Cleveland location, and we figured out how to kill it.
- Once we killed the dragon we achieved our potential.
- You probably have the same dragon in your location, and we can show you how to kill it so that you can achieve your potential too.
- Can we show you how to hunt and kill your dragon?

Here's the good news. You don't need many converts. In this example, if you can get a couple of branch locations outside of Cleveland to try out your prototype solution to increasing light bulb sales, and if those branch locations experience success with your prototype, then the word will spread on its own through the informal communication network in your business.

We have a saying in Texas that goes something like this: "Pioneers get shot and settlers get rich." In other words, nobody wants to be anybody's first customer, especially with an untested prototype that they are not required to try. You will have to use all of your personal influence and persuasive ability to get a couple of branches to try your prototype. You will have to hold their hand through their own testing, and you will have to make adjustments to your prototype that don't work in their specific location quickly or they will chuck it completely. Win over a couple of locations, or a couple of departments, or a couple of other teams. Work with them through the learning curve of how to apply your prototype to their specific situation, debug your prototype in real time so that your solution works every time just for them. Then, you will be creating "settlers." Then, your solution will start taking hold. You are nearing critical mass as the word spreads throughout the middle management communication channels that a real fix is out there and working.

Then, seemingly out of the blue, a miracle will happen. An executive at headquarters will get wind of something going on in the field that did not emanate from her office. She will see it in the improved light bulb sales numbers that are being generated by branch locations that have adopted and adapted your prototype. She will hear it through the formal reporting structure, as branch location managers tout their progress, on what was previously believed to be unsolvable problem. And she will hear through the rumor mill of a band of status quo insurgents, creating their own solutions to a problem once believed to be unsolvable.

Down the hall another executive, a politically competitive executive to our first executive, has also gotten wind of your prototype's adoption and results. Far from stomping it out, these competing executives will rush to see who can co-opt your solution the fastest. One of them will run to you and your team with open arms, notes of congratulations and maybe even a bonus or stock options, and then they will make the initiative their own and drive it into the rest of the business. This is the way the business world works, and it is a good thing as long as you stay focused on the objective–radical impact and the death of the dragon–and don't focus on your ego's need for a parade, though we all really want to throw you one. You absolutely must allow and encourage your prototype and its early converts to get sucked up into the vortex of executive ownership and initiative. No executive will take this prototype on unproven. Most executive are "settlers" and staunch supporters of the status quo. On the flip side, no executive wants to be left on the farm or in the fort when the final blow is dealt to the status quo dragon. When one of them sees that what you and your team are doing works and is being adopted, they will grab it and make it their own. By doing that, your prototype will be driven into the rest of the business by edict, policy, and program, and it will realize the full potential of its radical impact. The final blow to the dragon, the one that snuffs him out, occurs when you hand over the sword, and allow the trophy to be displayed in the co-opting executive's office. That's how it happens. That's how you finish off the dragon, by giving away the credit.

When you do that, when you finish off the last gasp of the status quo, you have concluded an epic development cycle in your middle management career, and whether you realize it or not, you have indelibly transformed yourself in the journey through the radical IMPACT cycle. That's the real payoff. Yes, you handed over one project to one executive at one point in time. Yes, she took the credit and she has the dragon's head hanging over her desk. But you are the hunter. You have worked through the radical IMPACT cycle. You are mastering strategic execution and you are the better for it. Over the rest of your career you will set forth on dozens if not hundreds of these types of radical impact hunts. You are the one transformed, not the executive. You are the middle manager who has joined the Order of I AM, and it will change everything for you going forward.

THE RADICAL IMPACT ORGANIZATION

I am sure that, by now, as you transition your first prototype into the larger business, that you have become abundantly aware of the limitations in your organization. The status quo is a powerful and entrenched foe and it has a one-hundred-year head start on you. Middle management as an empowered, creative group of radical impact hunters is an idea that has risen only recently, in the second century of management. It is really an idea that has only received serious inquiry in the last ten years or so. That means the brain-killing, cubicle nation-building, conformity school of management with a motto of "Shut up and do what we tell you to" has had a long time to dig in and establish its farms and fortresses. Don't be discouraged. Be grateful that you are managing in a time of transition, if you will lead it, if you will commit to hunting down the status quo and obliterating it.

The business you work for now, and the company you may work for tomorrow, likely is not structured to support radical impact-hunting. They are set up in the old way, the command and control, dehumanizing way, in a top-down vertical organization chart. That is where we need a radical transformation in the way businesses are organized and operate.

You have the courage and tenacity to work through the radical IMPACT cycle in your company and achieve radical impact even if your company does not modify the way it is organized and operates your journey will be an isolated experiment. You may personally benefit through a raise or promotion. You certainly will benefit from the new radical impact hunting skills you will have acquired. But in all reality, your isolated radical impact kill will not fundamentally change the culture of your organization. It will be one brick in a foundational shift that needs to occur, but it won't be complete.

For the organization to fundamentally shift foundations and unleash the potential of the middle, the top (the board, the ownership team, the big honchos) must lay in a radical impact engine into the organizational structure proper to force the move from a century's worth of status quo toward the potential for real radical impact. What I know, you know, and your top management knows, in their gut, is that real radical impact, earth-shattering, game-changing radical impact must come from the middle managers of the company. You and your peers are the radical impact engine of sustainable change that matters, the radical impact hunters who have the skill and staff to create real results that matter in your business.

So what does that organizational change look like? How do we organize a company that is structured to hunt down status quo dragons and kill them? How do we structure a company so that radical impact is what we do?

First, we have to tear down some of the hierarchical structure–not all of it, but some of it. We can't all dress up in togas and run around the woods doing whatever our heart leads us to do. That would be a recipe for chaos and bankruptcy. We do have to maintain some structured decision authority, organizational norms of behavior, and strategic vision from the thirty-thousand-foot level. But that's where I believe we can ditch the rest of the hierarchical organization chart that Mother Drucker was sold to us in the mid-twentieth century.

The straight pyramid organization chart is, by definition and design, a status quo-defending dragon. Over the last century the pyramid has sucked creativity and empowerment to the top level of the pyramid and left the rest of the structure to follow the manual and not cause trouble. Since the top of the pyramid is the source of all creativity and power in the company, then the rest of the pyramid is there to serve the top of the pyramid. This organization has a real cost, so we developed the most dehumanizing term in business to manage that cost and support effort, human resources. From the perspective at the top of the pyramid, you, in middle management, are a cost and a resource, like the raw materials you use to make your products, or the invoice you get from the landscaping company. So when times get tight in the company, the human resources team visits the middle and bottom of the pyramid and eliminates the cost through layoffs or other games of subtraction.

You are no longer a resource. You are the reason, and it is way past time that organizations recognize that and put structure to it. Human resources should have a name change to Human Reasons. Their mission should move from managers of benefits and compensation toward curators of inside-the-business genius. They should be the group feeding you knowledge and shouting out through the company newsletter every effort made to create radical impact. The Human Reasons department should champion time for you to spend on radical impact creation and build compensation structures to reward middle managers who use this time to create sustainable results that matter for the business.

To support this Human Reasons department, a new "C"-level executive should be added to every company that has any "C"-level executives at all. This "C"-level executive would be called the "Chief Performance Officer." Her job would be to organize and lead a perpetual radical impact hunt in the company. This CPO would have the authority to pull anyone in the company into a hunt team and could use up to one day of these people's capacity per week in the effort. The CPO would patrol across functional departments rooting out and obliterating the dragons of the status quo. One month they may be neck deep in the revenue-producing side of the business another they might be optimizing profitability. Whatever it takes to drive radical impact, the CPO would do it. She would answer to the CEO or board only, and her radical impact would be epic.

This simple shift in organizational structure, re-missioning HR, and adding the CPO function would drive greater collaboration both vertically and horizontally through the current organizational structure. It would tap the power of the middle management team and exponentially increase the rate of internal innovation in the company. It would speed up and decentralize the radical IMPACT cycle so that a wide range of prototypes could be occurring all the time in the business. Working through the radical IMPACT cycle work would become part of the DNA of this business.

We could stay the way we are with a pyramid hierarchy that sucks the energy to the top of the business. We have long since solved the challenges of staff compliance. Our people know how to keep their head down. The tight, rigid bureaucracy of a century-old structure has long since solved keeping everyone in their place. But doesn't that just seem stale in this age of unlimited human potential? Can't we use the pyramid hierarchy for its proven strengths and with a slight modification do nothing less than liberate our business? This modification in the age-old hierarchy would unlock and unleash the brainpower of middle management, and the result would be a business that is more creative, adaptive, and agile. That is a company geared up for the hunt on a constantly shifting frontier.

THE NEXT HUNT

In that first century of management, you were removed from the equation and transformed from the creative force of change you were designed to be, into a machine cog.

But you are more than that. The Vitruvian Principle taught you that in order to manage in a way that creates impact, achievement, and meaning, you must engage both the artistic and scientific nature of your very being. You were made to do this. When we consider each of our potential, we human beings are something to marvel at.

At the end of your first pass through the radical IMPACT cycle, with your first dragon kill notched on your belt, you will have entered the Order of I AM, a full card-carrying member. This simple act of changing your individual game is an act of great faith in yourself.

Now is the time to take up your sword and begin the radical IMPACT cycle anew. Do not rest. Do not admire. Hunt.

Your journey toward strategic execution mastery has only just begun. You will need to practice the radical IMPACT cycle dozens, if not hundreds, of times for it to become second nature. Your goal is mastery, sustained and meaningful mastery. You are your own radical impact project now. With each radical IMPACT cycle you complete, and with each team you engage, the ranks of the radical impact hunters grows. The life of the radical impact hunter is the life of the next hunt. Each day you awaken and undertake this challenge causes legions of status quo dragons to shudder in their caves.

They should.

RADICAL IMPACT

PART 3:
THE VITRUVIAN YOU

On your initial journey through the radical IMPACT cycle, you created out of nothing a sustainable result that matters in your business. That result is your masterpiece! Whether you realize it or not, you have begun developing higher-level Vitruvian characteristics. These are the traits that make great artists, scientists, and middle managers. With just one pass through the radical IMPACT cycle, a Vitruvian You begins to take form. These characteristics will continue to develop as you make more journeys through the radical IMPACT cycle.

You can build on the new Vitruvian You to establish yourself as a true business leader. You are a leader because of what you do not because of what someone calls you. Your willingness to join the hunt is what hones these characteristics and allows you to live a middle management life of impact, achievement, and meaning (I AM).

There are five radical leadership characteristics that separate true Vitruvian business leaders and radical impact hunters from farmers and fort dwellers. The five characteristics are the following:

COMMITMENT

CURIOSITY

COLLABORATION

CRAFT

COACHING

In this final part of the book, we take a reflective and contemplative look at these five characteristics that define the new and ever-evolving Vitruvian You. Take a moment to absorb the "war stories" in this section and use them as touchstones in your own journey toward a middle management life of impact, achievement, and meaning.

TEN: COMMITMENT

I was in a meeting of operations professionals in their company conference room. We were cloistered off from the rest of the business in the warehouse mezzanine. For five days I had been working through educating them in "deep dive" strategic execution techniques. These professionals were learning tangible techniques they could employ to drive radical impact through their departments and their own individual efforts.

Understand that you have never heard of this company, and you likely never will. Most of the companies with which I work–and most of the companies across the globe for that matter–aren't sexy, and most middle managers don't make the media headlines and features. Behind every public-facing and headline-grabbing company–WalMart, Amazon, Google–are thousands of mid-size industrial companies that sell products and services to each other. They pump an enormous amount of money into the economy and employ millions of people. The odds are pretty good that if you're reading this book you work for a company whose customers are other companies. That's the kind of company this company was.

As these professionals and I were wrapping up our two days of "deep dive" intensive education, most people in the room were shutting down their laptops, checking their iPhones, closing up their notebooks, all in attempt to let me know that even though I might not be done teaching, they were certainly done learning. Janine was the exception. She wasn't even supposed to be in the sessions. She was a last-minute addition because her boss couldn't make it, and he asked her to sit in on his behalf and take notes. There she sat, at the end of the conference table, with her hands resting on a pad of paper with and her head down. She was trying to hide the fact that she was crying. From the front of the conference room, I noticed that she was the only one in the room not packing it in.

So I asked Janine if she had a question.

She looked up, a line of tears running down her cheeks. She shook her head.

Other people in the room stopped their exit routine. One of the other women in the class put down her notebook, sat down next to Janine, an arm around her shoulder.

"I'm sorry," Janine said to the woman.

"Look," I said, trying to lighten the mood, "I know this material is challenging, but you will get it with time and practice. I promise."

She let out one of those half-laugh half-cries like kids let out when they realize they're not as hurt as they thought they were. "I'm not worried about that. I understand the material. I just got emotional because I began to realize that if I master this material and really do it, then I can really control my own future. I will be a pro."

That comment stopped the room. Then she looked at all her peers in the room to make sure that she had their attention.

"This stuff is a really big deal. Do you all see that?"

Left there, Janine's realization that mastering strategic execution could empower her entire career would have been enough to give us all a great feeling. But she did not leave it there. At that time, Janine, a middle-aged single mother, held a position as a clerk in the company. She was sent into the session to take notes for a disinterested boss. Over the next year, Janine immersed herself in the deliberate practice everyone must do to master strategic execution.

Did she put in extra hours to perform this practice? Yes. Was it a juggling act in her job responsibilities and parenting responsibilities to perform this practice? Yes. During this year did she have work-life balance? No. Did she "break" her kids or fail in her job responsibilities during that year of intense personal development? No.

But one year later, she was a manager, leading a team, making enough money to put her son through college. One year later she owned her life and was living it with deep sense of impact, achievement, and meaning. She entered the Order of I AM. Empowered, she was 100% a professional. She was not wealthy but she had broken free from the hold of the status quo.

Janine was just a clerk in a company you have never heard of in an industry you don't know exists. Yet her life and the lives of those around her were radically impacted by an awareness and follow through on her commitment to master strategic execution, to become a radical impact hunter. And it changed everything for her, her family, and her company.

MASTERY REQUIRES DELIBERATE PRACTICE

As you exit your first journey through the radical IMPACT cycle, you will have already achieved a level of commitment that many of your peers will not achieve throughout their entire career. This book's promise has been simple but not simplistic: If you abandon the middle-management life of the fort and the farm and enter the radical IMPACT cycle, you will enter the empowering realm of mastery. To master radical impact hunting you must deliberately practice the radical IMPACT cycle and that takes commitment.

Mastery requires deliberate practice. In his book *Talent is Overrated,* Geoff Colvin distills the research on deliberate practice and mastery. He explains that deliberate practice

- Must be repeated
- Necessitates continuous feedback on results
- Requires considerable focused effort and concentration
- And is not much fun.

The radical IMPACT cycle is custom-designed for your deliberate practice in strategic execution. But it will take enormous commitment to go through it repeatedly until you can wield this sword with the force of expertise.

In this way, your commitment to radical impact hunting is not a results-based commitment, which is what we want from our business leaders, isn't it? In fact, a focus on fast results can short change your development as a true radical impact hunter. If you commit to deliberate practice, you will get the results. You will achieve the result of radical impact. You will wipe out a lot of status quo dragons over your career.

The commitment you must make is to experiment, to stumble, to work the radical IMPACT cycle, and the results will follow.

COMMITMENT BEATS PASSION

Don't confuse commitment with passion. The myth of the new has spent a lot of ink on finding your passion, living your passion, working your passion. A radical impact hunter's passion is impact, achievement, and meaning in her work. Her commitment is to work over her technique tirelessly until she can slay every status quo dragon she encounters in her career. Commitment is showing up when it gets hard, when it doesn't feel good. Passion is a sugar buzz while commitment is endless nutrition.

Sometimes your work gets co-opted by the higher ups. It happens in the real world. This is a good thing if your commitment is in the right place. To stick with the deliberate practice you must be committed to the development of your own excellence, not approval or rewards. You will not get a parade the first few times through the radical IMPACT cycle. You can't let that discourage you. You will work harder than anyone in your business, and you will not make any more money, get promoted faster, or get much recognition, not in the early days. If you commit to your own development of excellence, this will not discourage you. If you do not, it will crush you.

This is the path of the business "Vitruvian." Vitruvian radical impact hunters are the penultimate business artists and scientists, and it is the price you pay to be great at what you do. Seth Godin says that we must give up "dancing monkey treats" if we are to do meaningful work in the world. Shove your ego in the closet and grind, work, lift, chisel your way through the radical IMPACT cycle. When you come out of the other side as a radical impact hunter, you will have achieved the goal of impact, achievement, and meaning. You also will become the arbiter of your career. The rewards will come, and they will come at an accelerated pace. They may take a couple of radical IMPACT cycles to materialize, but they will come.

RAISE THE BAR ON YOURSELF

As you master the radical IMPACT cycle in your current job and current employer, you will find yourself wanting to slay stronger status quo dragons. Depending on the structure of your organization, this may or may not be possible. Becoming a radical impact hunter is no guarantee that your organization will continue to challenge you to greater achievement. That's when it is time to strike the tent and journey out to the next quest. You are neither morally nor contractually required to stay with your employer if that employer is no longer challenging you. That is a false commitment advanced by the myths od loyalty discussed in Part I. Instead, commit to a progressive set of challenges throughout your career. Fight tougher and more challenging dragons, or you will get bored. You are an empowered and capable middle manager roaming the edges of the frontier of business possibility.

You do not have enough time in one career to wait for your business to catch up with you. Commit to this career economy. Don't waste your time in a business that's in love with its dragon collection. If you have demonstrated your ability, then move on. There are businesses out there searching for radical impact hunters. Find them.

Commit to

- deliberate practice and mastery
- raise the bar on yourself
- manage your own career

That commitment will change everything for you, your family, and the businesses that hire you for the hunt.

Will you commit to deliberate practice and mastery?

Will you commit to lead by this example?

Will you accept the empowerment that mastery provides and commit to manage your own career?

How has your sense of commitment to your business, to your career, and to results that matter changed through your first journey through the radical IMPACT cycle?

ELEVEN: CURIOSITY

No matter what I am trying to help a business or a department fix, I inevitably get asked to go to lunch with a couple of people who will be, well, a problem. These people are going to be necessary to implement any change that we are lining out in the conference room meeting, but they have, over their tenure with the company, proven to be very resistant to any change that requires them, well, to change. They are status quo "glue."

What works, most of the time, is to re-engage their curiosity. Somewhere along the line they quit asking questions, quit challenging themselves to find out what they didn't know. They listened to the dragon who told them that the big answers were handled by the big shots and that they just needed to keep their head down and do their job.

"Get your routines down," the dragon tells them, "then fight to hang onto them. You are the only one who really knows what's going on anyway."

The problem in this one company I was working with and having such a lunch with was this: They couldn't fill orders for basic "bread and butter" items in their market segment. This was causing their established customers to go to a competitor to fill their needs. The two people sitting across from me were the purchasing agents responsible for buying and positioning those "bread and butter" items in the correct distribution facilities across their region. The question is obvious, isn't it? So I asked it.

"Do either of you know why your business can't fill orders for bread-and-butter items?"

"No."

"Do you know that your business is losing customers because it can't fill orders on bread-and-butter items?"

"Yes, of course we do. Greg [the CEO] has sent us about a thousand emails on this."

"How do you respond to those emails?" I asked.

"We don't." "Do you think if you put your heads together you could figure out what the system is doing wrong?"

"Probably. But no one has ever asked us to do that."

If you are going to lead and continually deliver radical impact to businesses, then you must be curious. No question can be unworthy of inquiry. You must ask, and ask, and ask some more. The status quo wants you in the routine.

"Why must this be so?" is the beginning of the end of the status quo, and you must have the courage and engagement to ask it.

Ninety percent of the radical impact opportunities in your business can be solved within the walls of the business. You don't need gurus and you don't need consultants. You need to engage your curiosity and dig for answers. If your job has become mind numbing drudgery, the antidote is curiosity. You must develop a high level of curiosity to become the leader we need you to be.

How do you do that?

There are four key practices that you can employ to develop high levels of curiosity.

READ OUT OF YOUR COMFORT ZONE

Read anything and everything. The great thing about this information age that we are a part of is that you can find written information on just about any topic you can think of. Reading is, by its very nature, an act of curiosity. Picking up a book or a magazine, reading a blog post or online article is a pop in the mouth to the status quo. Google searches cannot solve radical impact, but it can get you started down a series of questions that will help you solve for radical impact. Obviously, I am a big fan of book-length reading. I tend to read about a book a week. But I don't limit myself to business books. Remember the Vitruvian Principle: Middle management is as much art as science. It is a balance of the two that makes you a radical impact hunter. Therefore, you can be informed in your middle management life by all kinds of subject matter outside of the business world. I learned a lot about sales management by learning to operate sail boats. The learning transferred from one topic to the other.

"Selling Against the Wind," "Growing Sales when the Market Tide Turns," you get the idea.

Incidentally, I learned to sail boats by reading books on sailing too.

Most of you quit reading or have a greatly diminished reading schedule since you completed your formal education. Build a list of topics that interest you in your business and start reading. This will feed your curiosity and keep you out of mind-numbing routines.

ENGAGE YOUR PEERS

Second, engage with your peers. One of the biggest killers to curiosity is isolation. If the status quo can keep you holed up in your cubicle, work group, department, or business, then it can trick you into thinking that you know everything there is to know. But if you will associate and engage with like-minded people outside your cubicle, work group, department, or business, you will maintain awareness that there are an infinite number of solutions and issues in the world to engage in, and you will maintain a curious mind. Here again, the information age helps us out. Find a "long tail" niche group or community online and engage in the discussion. Somewhere out there is a group of people in a physical or online community that does exactly what you do for a living. Plug into that group, engage in the discussion, and stay curious.

CARE

Along with engaging with your peers is the idea that curiosity is fed when you take a genuine and authentic interest in other people's well-being. Empathy feeds curiosity. This interest can be exercised anywhere, with your peer group, your staff, or your boss. The key is that it must be genuine interest. You know the difference, and it can keep your curiosity engine running.

I once worked with a staff that had a member who was having a difficult time finding an affordable education solution for her autistic grandson. The leader of that team engaged the whole group into researching and finding funding solutions to this challenge. Was that a business problem? No, not in the purest ideological sense of what a business problem is. But, when the team arrived at a funding solution for her grandson's education, they solved for a couple of things. One, they stayed curious and held onto that optimistic idea that every problem can be solved. Two, they really helped someone on our team. Three, as these team members move on in their careers, they will have a ready resource should this challenge come up with their staff members in the future. All of this benefit derived from a genuine and authentic interest in people's well-being. Selfishly, it helps us stay curious. Unselfishly, it can really help a lot of people.

LEARN FOR LEARNING'S SAKE

Finally, curiosity is kept alive when you learn for learning's sake. Explore anything you find you are interested in. I learned how to run a home-based recording studio once, not for money, not for any real practical reason, other than just because it was interesting to me. Becoming an autodidactic, someone who can teach themselves, is an exponential force for curiosity and a nuclear bomb to the status quo. The status quo wants you to believe that to learn you must be taught and certified, formally. If you can teach yourself then you beat that myth. If you can teach yourself by staying curious there is nothing you cannot learn your way through, which means there is no business problem you cannot solve.

Think about that for a minute. If you are curious, if you read, engage your peers, take an authentic interest in other people's well-being, and learn for learning's sake, there is not a business problem you cannot solve. That is a personal game changer, and that is at the heart of radical impact hunting.

What happened after my lunch meeting with the two purchasing agents? They got curious, maybe out of fear for their jobs, but they got curious nonetheless. They went back to their business, dug into the literature on their system, and read everything they could find on improving fill rates on bread-and-butter items. They engaged in a user group that helped them shortcut some of their experimentation with lessons the group had already learned. They met with sales teams so that they could get an authentic understanding of the challenges they faced on a day-to-day basis. Then, they committed to each other to develop a deeper understanding of purchasing techniques in their industry through self-paced online learning. And it paid off. Within a few months orders were being filled and customers started coming back, because two purchasing agents got curious.

Now that you have made your first journey through the radical IMPACT cycle, do you find that your curiosity has been re-engaged? Do you find yourself framing more "we could___if we___" statements? How has your curiosity improved with other staff members?

TWELVE:
COLLABORATION

There was a lot weighing on Allen's mind. It had been a tough year in the business of selling repair parts to capital equipment operators. The recession had caused belt tightening across the customer base, and what had hit him and his business the hardest was the massive reduction in repair parts budgets. Equipment operators were willing to let their machines go idle or operate sporadically in order to save money on parts, parts they bought from Allen's company. He had tried everything he could think of to stoke the fires of sales, but nothing had worked. He was staring straight down the barrel of a twenty-five-percent contraction in his company's size, and he dreaded the next decision he would have to make, layoffs.

Allen knew it was time to find solutions. He decided to gather a group of leaders in his business to brainstorm. Even this decision gave him concern. He had led several solutions sessions in the business over the years, and the results were consistently less than he had hoped for going into the session. It seemed like the sessions he had led in the past either devolved into a minor tweaking of management actions that had been taken in the past, became a defensive turf war, or the group simply agreed with what he was proposing. What Allen really wanted was to facilitate a discussion about a range of management actions that were new and innovative in an egoless, turf-less, safe room, a collegial discussion, where he was not only a facilitator, participant, and final arbiter, but also an equal in the session.

He had been trained to believe that a consensus solution was necessary to pull his company out of the steep decline it was in, but he was skeptical that his management team could come together in a way that would be effective. He was right to be skeptical. He brought his normal team of sales and marketing leaders together and posed the challenge to them. They spent two days locked in a room trying to solve a way to change the revenue trajectory of the company. At the end of the two days, this group of business leaders had decided that the key to their improved future was to give away free flashlights with their logo on it. That was the only action they could come to consensus on.

You should be shaking your head right now, because knowing no more than you do about this company and what it does, your gut tells you that logo flashlights are not going to fix their sales challenge. No, their revenue did not improve. But they all left the meeting feeling good, arms locked, in a consensus action. Allen knew at that point that his team, and its ability to drive any real radical impact into the business, was fundamentally limited.

Leaders who collaborate well get amazing things done in business, in politics, in all walks of life. The issue that has thrown us off course for the last ten years or so is that we confuse collaboration with consensus. This was the mistake Allen made in his company. His efforts at innovative solutions continually fell short because he spent his effort on consensus-building when he should have been collaborating.

We have become hyper-inclusive in our management style. This is in part due to the tomes of literature on change management that preaches that you must get consensus to have meaningful change "stick" in a company. The advice, while sounding good, does not work at scale or at speed. Our business environments are changing too fast, with too many moving parts, to generate consensus before we make any significant moves to the left, right, up or down.

Keep in the front of your mind at all times that most of the people in your business want to defend the status quo. Some of them, the more adventurous types, may venture into optimizing the status quo. Few of them, very few of them, want to create real radical impact. Without the innovators you are wasting your time collaborating. With the non-innovators, you will at best achieve some sort of incremental improvement of the status quo. At worst you will talk yourselves out of doing anything at all and will leave the status quo firmly in place.

You must collaborate to achieve radical impact. I want you to have radical impact, creating a sustained result that matters in your business. So let me give you the three key guidelines for radical impact collaboration.

OBLITERATE SOFTBALL COLLABORATION

Don't invite people to collaborate with you and your team because of their position on the organizational chart or their propensity to throw professional fits if they are left out of your think tank. Invite only the very most qualified people you can garner into your collaborative solution sessions. You absolutely must have the smartest people on the topic you can get. This may mean going to a shipping clerk if you are solving a logistics challenge, or it may mean going to the president of the company if you are solving a market segment challenge. You have to be fearless here. Your effort to create radical impact is too important and urgent to waste time on the "look" of your collaborative group.

COLLABORATORS DO THEIR HOMEWORK

Second, if you are going to enter the realm of real hardball collaboration, your collaborative team members have to do their homework and understand that their ideas will be vetted and scrutinized. The reality is that some people just don't have the stomach for the radical impact hunt. Their egos aren't strong enough to advance an idea into a collaborative team, have it torn up, and then revise the idea based on feedback and come back at it. That takes a lot of persistence and a lot of radical leadership trait number one, commitment.

When I worked at General Electric, there was a training course at their world-class training facility in New York called "Management Development Course." Everyone knew it as "MDC," a coveted course. If you were selected to attend "MDC," that meant that the higher ups at GE had designated you as a high potential manager (a "high pot" in the GE vernacular). That designation, along with completion of MDC, was a career maker inside GE. At the end of MDC, teams of attendees would be put into the "pit." The "pit" was a sunken ring-shaped floor in an arena-style classroom. When you or your team were in the "pit," you and your team's project assignment was subject to a withering series of inquiries from the attendees and guests in the class. Sometimes, Jack Welch himself would attend and participate in these examinations. In the "pit" not only were your ideas and solutions being vetted and scrutinized; your ability to handle the assault also was being observed by the instructors. If you crumbled, and more than a few people did, then there were real career negative implications.

Sound too tough?

Too brutal?

I wish I could make this journey easy, but I can't. Radical impact is about middle managers creating a sustainable result that matters in a business. This act of creation is in direct defiance to the status quo dragon that lords over most companies. You cannot go into battle with that dragon half-prepared, partially vetted, or under-scrutinized. That dragon will expose every weakness you and your collaborators have as it attempts to thwart your effort and hold the status quo in place. It is far better and far more diligent to vet and scrutinize each other in the safety of the "small conference" room than it is to be obliterated in the field by the fire of the status quo's defense. GE understood that if you couldn't survive the "pit," which was a simulation, then you didn't stand a chance in the real business environment. Conversely, if you could get through that test, and if you and your collaborators will impose the same self-inflicted crucible, you will be one hell of a force to be reckoned with.

COLLABORATORS MUST WEIGH IN

Third, being part of a collaborative solutions team is not a check box. You must have collaborators who will participate in the collaboration. You will waste valuable hours inviting collaborators into the room, only to watch them take a few notes, and never say a word. They may be smart, qualified, and able, but if they don't jump in, they are of no help to you. The radical IMPACT cycle is the cauldron, the crucible, the testing ground of ideas. Groups come up with much broader solutions than individuals if they are qualified group members and if they speak up. You might have to force feed this participation process early, especially if your collaborators don't know you well enough to trust you yet.

Here's an example. I was leading a national supply chain and had just finished a month's worth of work on my operating plan for the next year. It was, in my mind, the best plan I had ever put together, yet I knew it was completely born out of my homework and my perspective. I had identified a great team of collaborators whom I wanted to vet and scrutinize my plan. I told them the plan.

This operating plan is a draft, I told them. It is not cast in stone. It is not precious, and it is not brilliant. I asked them to take four weeks and review the plan with this mindset—there is no way that this operating plan will work. "Build your arguments as to why this plan won't work," I said, "and be prepared to share them in our session in four weeks."

The team I had gathered to collaborate was unforgiving. They did exactly as I asked and tore my operating plan to shreds. They participated, collaborated, and added an enormous amount of value to the operating plan quality. After their candid scrutiny, the plan was revised, the weak points shored up, and we had a great year.

CONSENSUS IS NOT COLLABORATION

There is a drill in the Marine Corps called the "hand grenade drill." Our team would be traipsing through the woods on a simulated patrol and the instructor would throw a smoke grenade into the group. The smoke grenade was harmless, but it was there to simulate the real thing, which was definitely not harmless. Whoever saw the smoke grenade first yelled out, "Grenade!" at which point the rest of us dove toward the nearest thing that could protect us, a tree stump, a rock, whatever we could find. This drill taught us that in a crisis the most effective course of action is to follow the lead of the first person to assume decisive leadership.

"Grenade!" is no time to gather thought leaders and build consensus on which way to dive, who should dive first, and what dives worked in the past. You get dozens of

"Grenade!" attacks in your business every day, and you get blown up while building consensus. Consensus is a lethal way to make decisions. That's what leaders are for, to make decisions. You need the group to innovate and collaborate, but they stink at making decisions.

Don't confuse consensus with collaboration. Disregard most consensus in the radical IMPACT cycle. In the radical IMPACT cycle, concentrate on collaboration. Build a collaborative group of qualified individuals who have thick enough skin to have their thoughts and ideas scrutinized. Encourage, and demand if necessary, participation in that scrutiny, and make sure you are thick-skinned enough for it as well. Use collaborative groups effectively and you will be demonstrating a radical leadership trait characteristic very few middle managers have the stomach to employ.

As you have collaborated with your team through the radical IMPACT cycle, when and how did collaboration help you solve a pressing issue or show the "way" forward?

THIRTEEN: CRAFT

When my son was four years old, he asked me to coach his soccer team. I had grown up playing soccer. My sister was good enough to play soccer on a college scholarship. So, I thought I had the competency to coach a group of enthusiastic four year olds. We practiced the skills you need to develop as a soccer player, ball handling, passing, positioning, and that was all fine and good. These four year olds actually practiced really well. But then came game time. Once the whistle blew to start the game, these four year olds, who had been taught well, bunched up into a ball like frantic bait fish. The other team reacted the same way, and I am sure their coach taught his team the same skills I had taught mine. It was discouraging. Despite our practice on spacing and positioning, when game time came, every one of those four olds panicked and reverted back to their gut instinct which boiled down to, "Everyone run after the ball and scream."

Yes, they were only four and, yes, they were having fun.

I, like many sports fans around the globe, am entranced by the every four-year spectacle of World Cup soccer. All of the teams employ a set of soccer skills that are world-class. Their ball handling is acrobatic, their passing, precise, and their positioning, bordering on the clairvoyant. They are true craftsmen at their chosen profession. That is how the game should be played.

But every player on every World Cup team was, at one time in their life, running after the ball and screaming with a group of four-year-old boys.

The difference between those World Cup soccer experts and the rest of us is nothing more and nothing less than mastery of craft, and craft takes a lot of sustained and focused effort to develop.

CRAFT BROADENS SOLUTIONS

In middle management, we are quick to run after the ball and scream. The business drives us to panic, and when pressed, we deploy brute force solutions to solve the problems in front of us. Often, in our four-year-old soccer mode, we 1)add staff, 2)cut staff, 3)add stuff, or 4) cut stuff, to every problem we encounter. This deployment of exactly four techniques is nothing more than running after the ball and screaming. It is middle management by brute force.

There is no craft here. This is survival management. This is "get-the-boss-off-my-back management." This is "make-it-the-other-guy's problem management." And you and I know that this is the style of play that rules the day in most of our businesses, "Hey, everybody! Grab a cup of coffee, and then let's all run around and scream for the rest of the day."

Strategic execution, when mastered through deliberate practice of the radical IMPACT cycle, will transform you into a world-class middle manager with a wide range of deployable tactics to solve business's toughest problems. But to be that adept, you must constantly work on the trade craft of middle management. The world really needs you to get good at this, but it takes time. And lack of time, or the perception of lack of time, is a trick the dragon uses to keep you from getting good at what you do. As long as you and everyone in the office just run around and scream, the status quo will always and forever win the day.

"IN" THE BUSINESS, "ON" THE BUSINESS

There is work in the world that you (and only you) can do, if you could only get to it. Your day is consumed with the status quo conspiracy of working "in" the business at the expense of working "on" the business. The dragon is keenly aware of anyone who makes any attempt to break out of the fort or the farm. As soon as you strike out, you are a threat. So, the dragon has devised a neat little trick called the daily crises. Here's how the daily crisis works to thwart your early efforts at radical impact.

You might start your day with an intention to practice the radical IMPACT cycle. Maybe you are early in an inquiry that you believe could lead to a radical impact solution. It's early, but you are on the scent. You have decided that today you will spend the first two hours of the day in a deep dive inquiry. Wide awake, the dragon throws an email at you from your director. The email is in all capital letters, with words that have been emboldened, italicized, and underlined. This must be critical. So, without discussion with your director around the importance of his work versus yours, you jump at his email. You abandon working "on" the business so that you can work "in" it. You are now in problem-solving mode, and it will easily eat up the rest of your day.

As you send out an email to your director at five o'clock, you promise yourself that you will get back into your deep dive inquiry first thing in the morning. After all, it's just one day that you lost. In the shadows the dragon is manufacturing an entire series of daily crises for you to solve. And before you know it, those "just one day" problem-solving efforts have turned into a week, a month, a year, or a career. Yes, I have seen middle managers spend their entire careers solving daily crises problems for the boss. These are people that the boss calls "the go-to managers." They are, supposedly, the people who keep the machine of the business running. They hold it all together through their daily hustle and effort working "in" the business. They are "the go-to managers," and they will forever be stuck in place. Their careers are nailed to the floor of their current role, destined to forever be someone else's problem-solver, troubleshooter. If you are forever working "in" the business and never "on" the business, then you will not get through enough radical IMPACT cycles to master the craft of strategic execution. The radical IMPACT cycle is not problem-solving in the day-to-day sense. The radical IMPACT cycle is performance-solving in the mid-to-long-term sense. It requires a different level of managerial trade craft to create a sustainable result that matters to a business versus keeping the boss off your back. True craft, radical impact hunting craft, has to be developed while working "on" the business, not "in" it.

Since the dragon perks up and prepares a plethora of distractions in your effort to work "on" your business and your managerial craft, you will have to develop some sneaky techniques to subvert the dragon's attempts to throw you into day-to-day problem solving. Craft mastery requires commitment followed by deliberate practice. This deliberate practice through the radical IMPACT cycle requires time.

20% TIME

Take a page out of Google and 3M's playbook. Those companies allow their programmers and engineers one day a week to work on anything they want. They get to experiment, code, design, fiddle, anything, as long as it has some outcome that could benefit the business. Google has even named this process "Twenty Percent Time." Gmail was developed in "twenty percent time" at Google, and "sticky notes" were developed in "twenty percent time" at 3M. Big stuff can come out of time spent developing your craft. Most of you are not programmers for Google or product development engineers for 3M. So, where are you going to get that "twenty percent time?"

You steal it.

You steal it from staff who aren't lifting a finger beyond the day-to-day.

Follow these simple directions, and you can create eight hours a week of time to deliberately practice your middle management craft through the radical IMPACT cycle.

First, make a list of ten things that you would have to eliminate from your "typical" day that would allow you to spend an hour and a half a day of sustained focused effort, no interruptions, on your practice in the radical IMPACT cycle. Take five minutes to produce this list. Don't over think it. Just make a list, fast.

Review your list and notice how many items are having more impact on your business in the mid- to long-term than if your were working through the radical IMPACT cycle to deliver a sustainable result that matters to your business. Circle the items in your list that are impacting the business less than you could if you delivered a sustainable result that mattered.

Here's the fun part. Next to each item you circled on your list, write the name of a person who could do these things. They may be peers, subordinates, or even the boss. Better yet, how many of these circled items could be eliminated altogether? Would the world end if you just stopped doing them? If you can eliminate these tasks, then write "eliminate" next to them. If you can't, then write someone's name down. Now, with all your charm, influence, authority, or creative begging, get them to take these tasks away from you. It will feel uncomfortable, but the stakes are too large to hide in your discomfort.

My guess is that you have freed up about eight hours per week. If you have not, then build another list, go through the same process until you have freed up those hours. Now, you can work on your craft. Now you can practice by working "on" the business, if you avoid yet another subtle trap that the dragon has laid for you.

Yes, that dragon knows how to suck up that eight hours before you ever get a chance to use them. How? By dangling your email's inbox in front of you.

You can already hear the dragon's whisper can't you?: "You don't need eight whole hours to work on the radical IMPACT cycle every week. You could use just one hour or two to get on top of your emails and then you would have even more time to work on radical IMPACT."

The assault is subtle and lethal. And it will trap you if you let it. You get nearly 12,000 emails a year. Just reading and mentally processing this volume of inbound stimulus can consume as much as fifty percent of your work day time. We can spend an hour or two a day just checking our inbox. In other words, we are spending hours a day just seeing if there is something we would rather be doing than what we are doing now.

Radical impact has never been achieved through a keen sensitivity and responsiveness to email. Get out of your inbox and into your trade craft. Use the time you cleverly acquired to do real work on your craft. The emails can wait.

A life of impact, achievement, and meaning is a life dedicated to craft. And the Vitruvian You is a master craftsman.

How will you carve out the time you need to develop your craft through deliberate practice?

How will you trade today's crises for development and dare to master your profession?

The status quo knows that middle management is the single greatest force for achievement in the business world today. And it will fight desperately to keep you from developing that force of craft. The challenge for you is to fight the illusion of time scarcity, claim it, use it, and become the middle management craftsman the world needs you to be.

FOURTEEN: COACHING

As you exit your first journey through the radical IMPACT cycle, you assume the position of subject matter expert. You know the "ins and outs" of this specific solution better than anyone. Embrace your role as subject matter expert. It is this implied authority that will give you the organizational horsepower to push your next solution into business. You will have to rally people around a solution they will resist, and then you will have to make sure they are executing the solution correctly so that it achieves radical impact. You have entered the realm of coaching.

Coaching is both a personal style of leadership and a hard-boiled set of techniques. Not all middle managers are coaches, but all radical impact hunters are. The best middle managers you have ever worked for were great coaches. The best teachers you ever sat in class with were great coaches. And if you were fortunate enough to have great parents, like

I was, they were also great coaches. Volumes and volumes of business and personal improvement literature have been written on the topic of coaching. I am not going to review or expound upon that body of knowledge here. Here, I am going to show you two status quo traps to avoid in coaching through the radical IMPACT cycle, discuss great coaching techniques, and show you the number one secret to great coaching.

As you push your team through the radical IMPACT cycle you will uncover all kinds of issues not originally chartered in your project scope. These issues can easily roll into the realm of challenges to your individual team mates, your staff, and the business at large. Since you will be digging, asking questions, and engaging in dialogue throughout the business, people will see you as a sympathetic ear and will use the opportunity to pour their problems into your lap. This is a status quo maneuver designed to throw you off the hunt, and many middle managers get sucked up in the trap. Coaching is not enabling.

SUSTAIN FOCUSED EFFORT

Your ability to radically change a piece of your business and create a sustainable result that matters relies on your sustained and focused effort. If you transition this role into advocating up the organizational chart or trying to solve everyone's individual problems, then you will never achieve radical impact. You will be loved and known as a great empathetic manager, a great human being, but you will not achieve radical impact. Your coaching effort must be laser-focused, on achieving radical impact through the project you have taken on. Your business and the people's issues within it are legion. You will not solve them now. Don't try.

COACH YOUR REPLACEMENT

On the other end of the spectrum, the status quo likes to trap you into not coaching at all. It does this by playing to your fear and to your sense of wasting time. On the fear side, the status quo whispers this lie into your ear: "You know, if you really develop Lance into the talent that he could be, then he just might replace you, and soon."

In General Electric we were told that there were three capable people waiting to take our job at any given moment. You probably have staff right now that with a little focused coaching could take over your job duties.

Does that make you nervous?

It shouldn't. You can't move up in the company if you have not trained your replacement. The succession gap caused by not having someone capable of doing my job cost me a couple of promotion opportunities early in my career.

My bad coaching technique at the time was to use staff to feed me knowledge and intelligence so that I was always the smartest guy in any meeting. That was all great and good until the business realized that I was an intelligence choke point, the only place in the business where anyone knew what was going on. I was stuck, not promotable, because I had not decentralized my knowledge and coached people up who could take my place.

If you are in a good organization, your ability to coach up your replacement will get you promoted quickly and often. Don't fall into the trap that your staff is nipping at your heels so you should keep them in the dark, dumb, and underdeveloped. That is coaching death. It is not the right way to work, you won't keep good talent, and you won't advance in your business.

COACHING STRENGTHENS YOUR TEAM

With the "new" economy and a younger generation of professionals, the days of staying in one company for your entire career are long gone. Even the idea of working in one specific job field your entire career is becoming dated. Employee turnover is a fact of life these days, and that brings another status quo assault to your ability as a coach.

Here's what the status quo tells you to get you to bail out: "You know, these kids today, they come and they go, they don't know what they want to do, but they know what they don't want to do, and that is anything you need them to do. Right? You could spend hours and hours coaching them up to speed, but then what? They are going to leave and you just trained your competitor! What a waste of time."

Is it a waste of time to invest hours, days, weeks, months, or years coaching people that have a better than even chance of leaving you?

Yes.

What if you don't coach them and they stay? Now what have you got? A drone?

COACHING IS UBER-NETWORKING

At the other end of the spectrum, from your own career management perspective, coaching in a high turnover economy is a backdoor way of networking. If your staff identifies you as a great coaching middle manager, and they leave your business (which they likely will), then you will have created an alumni network that will pull you to the next opportunity as well. Be generous with your staff. Give them everything you know. You are not wasting time. You are creating a strong network of supporters, and you are spreading the ability to create radical impact beyond the walls of your business.

As a manager of staff, you have signed up to be a coach whether you realize it or not, so be a great one. Bring each member of your team into your personal circle and develop a long-term career plan with them. This goes way beyond the annual performance review that we waste time on every year. Really get into the gut of your staff. They are individuals with life goals and dreams that you can help them achieve. Customize an individual development roadmap for every coachable person on your staff. This is not a role you can outsource to human resources. Why not?

Because if you fail to pull alongside your staff and work with them on a real development roadmap, you lose authenticity. Your staff craves authenticity. As you outsource to HR the one thing you can really help them with, you become a corporate mouthpiece, the boss. Real coaches own their relationship to their staff's goals and dreams. Think about that for a minute. To be a great coach, you must develop a relationship not only with your staff, but with their goals and dreams. Their goals and dreams have to mean as much to you as they do to them. That is authentic. Then, when authenticity is established, you can coach them through short, mid- and long-term goals and actions to achieve those goals and dreams. And when you achieve them together, you can celebrate together.

I have maintained coaching relationships with people who haven't worked for me in over a decade, and, no, they aren't paying me. The relationship we established as manager and staff was so real, authentic, and empowered that we have maintained it, and leveraged it, well beyond the time that we worked together. Are you willing to coach like that? How much does a staff member mean to you? Do you want them to do work for you, or do you want them to be great? There is so much you can achieve through others if you will commit to authentic coaching.

THE POWER OF EXAMPLE

What is the number one, hands-down, secret sauce to being a great coach in business?

Your example.

That's it. Those whom you coach will look at you and observe your behavior, your career, and your dealings with other people, more than they will listen to anything you have to say. Through your example you are either adding to or detracting from your authenticity as a coach in every minute of every day. I can think of an infinite number of examples where what a leader said he was going to do did not match his actions. I count on one hand the number of authentic coaches who have led me.

Coaching is nothing more and nothing less than having an authentic and structured relationship with your staff. Teach them everything you know. Share with them your passion for the hunt. Then watch as they strike out on their own toward the frontier of their capability, searching for status quo dragons of their own to conquer.

BEGIN

Middle managers, you have the innate potential to create radical impact in your businesses right now and change the way you work forever. This is the "call to arms" I issued at the beginning of the book, and you answered it. You left the false safety of the farm and the fort and set out on your first radical impact hunt. Then, you slayed the status quo dragon and created a sustainable result that matters in your business, radical impact, and joined the ranks of radical impact hunters. What you have experienced, through your first radical impact hunt is that the aspiration of a middle management life of impact, achievement, and meaning is as close to you as the next iteration through the radical IMPACT cycle. Strategic execution is a craft that you will master over time through an ever-evolving series of radical impact hunts. The Vitruvian You will emerge clearer and stronger after each successful conquest of the dragon of the status quo.

Radical impact is in front of you right now, in a question, in a step, in a new journey.

BEGIN.

ACKNOWLEDGEMENTS

This book would not have happened without the contributions and influence of a large group of people.

Thank you Ellen, Grant, and Zoe for all the support you have given me through the years. I couldn't do a thing without you.

Thanks to Mom and Dad for showing me that a family of managers can be rich with meaning if you keep the faith, work hard, and stick together.

Special thanks to the team at Tracking Wonder Consultancy (trackingwonder.com), especially Jeffrey Davis for his patient and thoughtful editing and coaching as well as Holly Moxley for her magical design.

The team at PKF Texas is a group of collaborative supporters I simply could not function without. Thank you, Karen, Raissa, and Jen for your generosity. Special thanks to Kenneth and Byron for your stalwart business support.

Thanks to Sherry Menger and Misty Morales for creating the space and support to get this book done.

Thanks to the "soundboard" brain trust of Matt Cook, Chris Wallace, and Jonathan Contre. You are all giants of business thought and execution.

Thanks to the original "Rads," Roger, Mike, Jon and Richard. You are where the "rad" road began.

Finally, there is no book on middle management impact, achievement, and meaning without the countless interactions I have had with countless middle managers throughout my career. There are too many of you to mention here, but I will take a swing at a few. Thanks to Luzanna, Lourdes, Erin, Jason, Jesse, Deb, Ken, Rocio, Chris, Raj, Craig, Joel, Eric, Neil, Marcos, Scott and John. It has been a pleasure working with you all. Keep hunting!

ABOUT THE AUTHOR

Andy Ray is Principal at PKF Texas. He is a practicing management coach, business consultant, and writer. He has advised a number of firms on middle management development and creating sustainable results that matter.

He lives in the Houston area and can be reached through www.PKFTexas.com.